With Purpose:
The Balmoral Standard

Traci Brooks, Carleton Brooks
with Rennie Dyball

Foreword by
PIPER KLEMM, PH.D.

THE PLAID HORSE

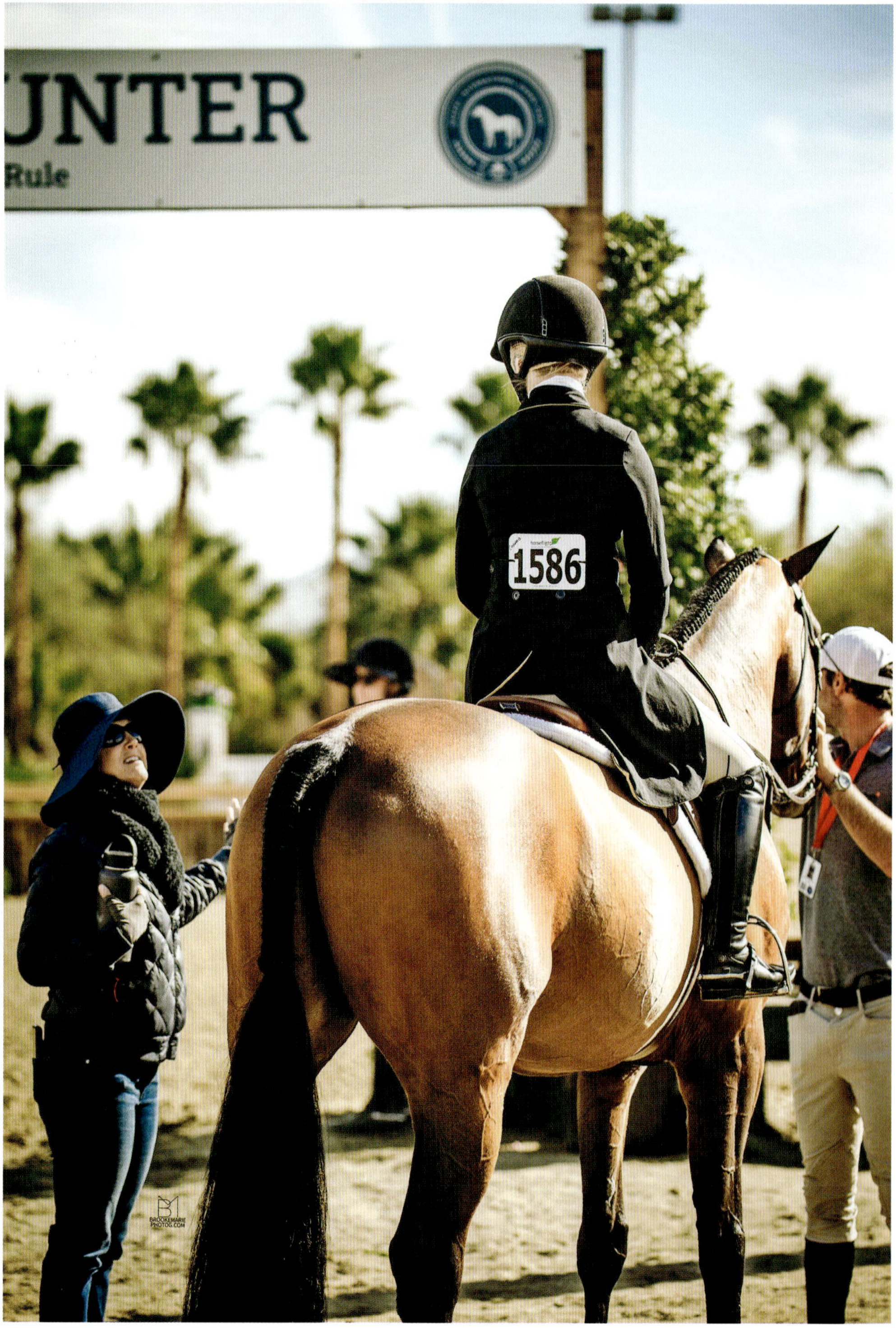
UNTER
Rule
1586
BROOKEMARIE PHOTOG.COM

CONTENTS

Advance Praise — 4
Foreword — 6

Part I: On Horsemanship — **12**

Chapter 1 The Horse Comes First — 14
Chapter 2 Care and Organization — 17
Chapter 3 Think Like a Horse — 33
Chapter 4 Establishing the Horse and Rider Relationship — 41
Chapter 5 Conformation — 45
Chapter 6 Tack and Equipment — 51
Chapter 7 Safety — 59

Part II: On Training — **66**

Chapter 8 The Importance of Forward — 68
Chapter 9 Notes on Flatwork — 87
Chapter 10 Notes on Jumping — 95
Chapter 11 "The Distance" — 103
Chapter 12 Routines for Riding at Home — 109
Chapter 13 Routines for the Horse Show — 117
Chapter 14 The Mental Game — 129
Chapter 15 Fear (a.k.a. The "F" Word) — 133
Chapter 16 Laugh at Yourself — 139
Chapter 17 Learning Out of the Saddle — 141

Part III: On the Industry — **150**

Chapter 18 Barn Culture — 152
Chapter 19 Our History with Horses — 157
Chapter 20 Through Each Other's Eyes — 165
Chapter 21 Working in the Hunter Jumper World — 169
Chapter 22 On Judging — 173
Chapter 23 Horse Insurance — 178
Chapter 24 Balmoral on Carleton and Traci — 185

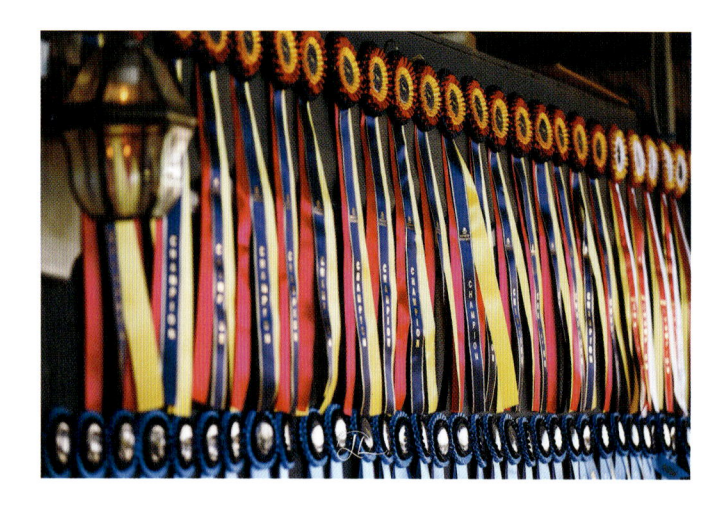

ADVANCE PRAISE FOR CARLETON AND TRACI BROOKS

"I've shown alongside Traci and Carleton for many years and have seen firsthand how they always put the horse first. That system produces happy, healthy animals, along with fulfilled riders and impressive horse show victories. Anyone who rides will learn so much from them by reading *With Purpose*."

—Leslie Steele

"I am so looking forward to reading Carleton and Traci Brooks's *With Purpose*. What I value most about what Carleton and Traci stand for is that they truly listen to and learn from the horses and the riders as individuals more than they simply copy what other trainers are doing. Sadly, in this day and age, this is unusual, and I look forward to learning new and valuable thought processes to implement in my own work."

—Geoff Teall, USEF "R" Judge, author of *Geoff Teall on Riding Hunters, Jumpers, and Equitation*

"Traci and Carleton Brooks embrace the whole horse and the whole rider. I have worked with them in my role as a mental skills coach for many years and it has been an honor to be part of their team. Their expertise, professionalism, and never-ending curiosity about how to help their athletes be their best is such an inspiration. I can't wait to read *With Purpose*!"

—Tonya Johnston, Mental Skills Coach

"It's hard to be a rider, a trainer, and a coach. A lot of people are good people trainers and not good horse trainers, a lot of people are good horse trainers and can't talk to people. Carleton can do all of that. He can train people, he can teach people, he can teach the horses, and then being a coach is even a different thing. You've got to know when to have a little iron hand, you've got to know when to feed them a little sugar. Carleton knows the right time to do all of it."

—Jack Towell, from Carleton's USHJA Lifetime Achievement Award ceremony

"Traci and Carleton Brooks have created a training program that produces results at all levels. Their philosophy, coupled with top-notch training and horse care, creates opportunities for horses and riders to thrive. Readers of *With Purpose* will gain insight into the Balmoral way in this interesting and highly educational guide."

—Frank Madden

"Team work truly makes the dream work. For the first time in my career, I had the privilege to work together with Traci and Carleton Brooks. It's amazing to see the process they take with developing their horses. The intricate attention to detail and obsession with finding the perfect formula to make their horses successful is something I really admired. I had so much fun developing Devon Grand Champion Hunter, Only Always, with both Traci and Carleton throughout the year. Collaborating with this power couple was such a great experience. Horsemanship, talent, and success—that's Balmoral."

—Nick Haness

"Traci and Carleton offer a look into what a power couple in the equestrian world is all about. They are not only amazingly talented, they are so kind and both willing to offer advice and support anytime it's asked. I'm lucky to have the opportunity to learn from them firsthand, and I am so excited for everyone to read this book and gain some insight on this amazing duo!"

—Nicole Bourgeois, trainer at Imagination Lane LLC

"CB is the ultimate horseman—he is all about the horse and its well-being. He can ride with the best of them—inside and outside the show ring."

—Susie Schoellkopf, USEF "R" judge

What exciting news to hear that Traci & Carleton Brooks will soon be releasing *With Purpose*. They combine the best traditions of classical horsemanship with the most current methods of care and training of modern sporthorses. Having watched their program and judged their horses for decades, their approach brings out the best in each individual horse and rider. They nurture and support that extra special quality that defines the highest caliber performance horses and riders. I'm especially excited that their insights will now be available to private farm owners as well as larger training barns. Good news!

— Connie Tramm Hunt, USEF "R" judge

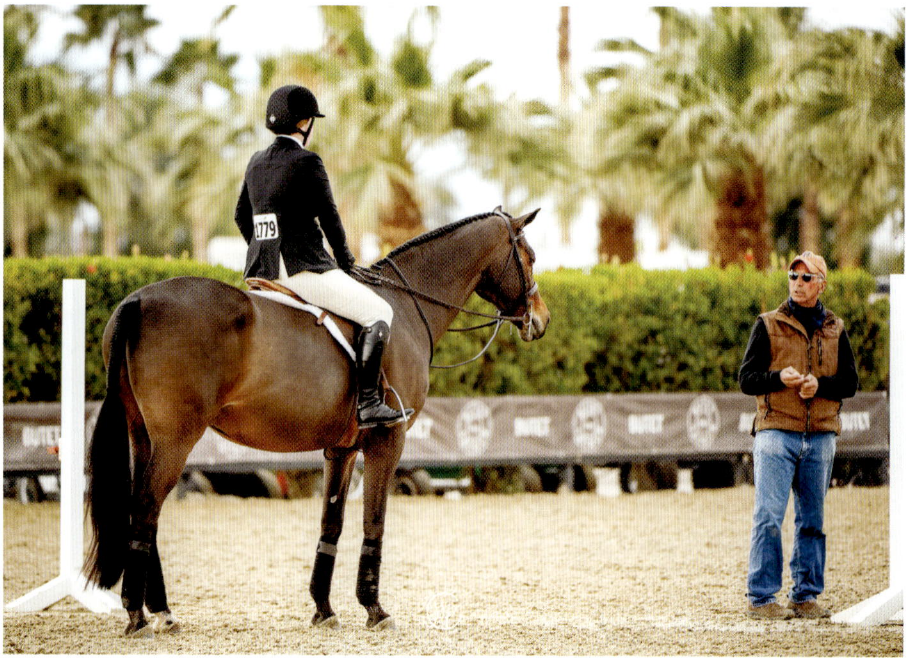
1779

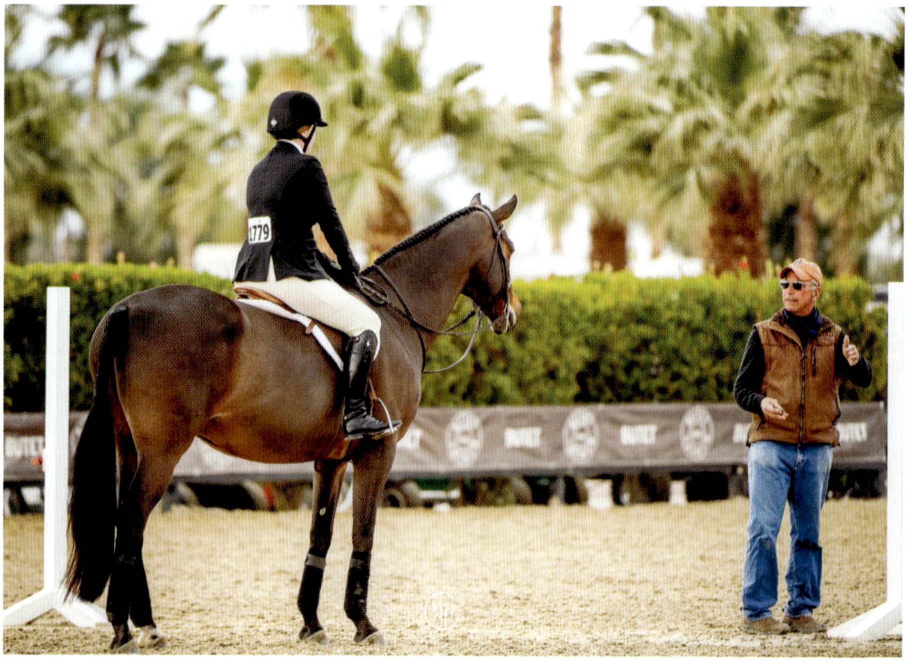
1779

FOREWORD

By Rennie Dyball and Piper Klemm

I FIRST MET Carleton, "CB" to those who know him, at Harrisburg in 2019. Piper introduced us at the Balmoral stalls to chat about the possibility of writing a book.

"What would the first chapter be?" he asked me. Carleton always asks good questions.

"That's up to you," I told him. "What is the most important thing you want to impart to readers?"

His reply was quick and simple. "The horse comes first," he said with a shrug, explaining that lots of people in our sport may say as much, but few truly act on it, day in and day out. "It's not about what happens in there," he added, gesturing in the direction of the ring. "It's about what happens here."

We talked a bit more, and then CB started to appear distracted, looking over my shoulder.

"That horse wants to stick his head out," he told me, pointing to a stunning bay gelding named Pritchard Hill, his ears pricked in our direction from inside his stall.

He does? I wondered. How could CB know that with just a glance?

As I'd come to learn over the next two years of working with Carleton, he just knows. It seems almost magical, but it's actually the result of decades spent putting the horse first. A glance is sometimes all it takes for a horseman dedicated to his own definition of horsemanship. You'll learn that definition in chapter one.

Unsurprisingly, Pritchard Hill did want to stick his head out. Carleton opened the stall door and clipped a stall guard in its place. The horse stepped forward and stretched his neck out, content to listen in on our conversation.

Like Carleton, Traci is unequivocally invested in all of Balmoral's horses, settling for no less than the very best in their care. But on a misty December morning at the West Los Angeles, California barn, she is like all of us, simply visiting with the horses she loves.

At each stall, Traci shares a little anecdote with me about the horse inside. Often, it's about what makes them special to her. She is magnetic to the horses—and to just about every person she meets. Warm and engaging, Traci has an uncanny knack for knowing exactly what a rider needs to hear. She meets every person where they are and tailors her training to get the most out of them. Watching her teach is truly a riding lesson.

Bringing together decades of experience, Traci and Carleton's knowledge is impressive, extensive, and—here's the best part—shareable. You cannot spend five minutes in their company (or with this book) without learning something new. I feel very lucky to have spent so much time with them at home and at the horse shows. My own riding, and more importantly my horsemanship, have improved, thanks to the lessons CB and Traci have taught me. Yours will, too.
—*Rennie*

❖❖❖

GROWING UP IN THIS SPORT, I always subscribed to luck. I had my lucky socks, and I was superstitious about the ordering of absolutely everything before I showed. Whether I might have success that day would come down to whether I had enough luck for the pony to be good, or for me to find the jumps. As I grew older and all this luck seemed to go to others, I became increasingly hard on myself and missed out on what I craved—being in the moment, enjoying the horses, and making strategic and good decisions for them.

I never sorted all of this out and focused on my own traditional education, which was defined and logical. I wound up years later by kismet at the in-gate with Traci and Carleton Brooks. I have stayed for the better part of the last decade because it has been the most fantastic and inspirational learning experience I could possibly imagine.

The first day I ever rode with Balmoral was the first day that I truly believed that this sport was defined and systematic. A system where I had control: I could control my mastery of it. I could control my learning. I could control my input.

That very first day I rode with Balmoral, I stood next to Carleton at Hunter Ring 6 at Thermal and he explained to me how to ride every stride of the course. Where to turn, what markers to look at, and where I should be turning my head and what I should be feeling. He told me how to put my leg on, where and when to pick my hands up. I remember thinking that this would be amazing if it worked. I so hoped it would as I put my foot in the stirrup.

While at that point he had never seen me ride, he knew his system and he knew his horse. In the schooling ring, he made two seamless adjustments to the plan when he saw weakness he could correct in a lap or two. He never pointed out anything we couldn't fix in the schooling ring. He was definitive and positive and sent me into the ring. While I was terrified by the magnitude of the opportunity of riding with Balmoral, and I was pretty sure I was going to screw up, I had these novel competing emotions of positivity and comfort that started to push that away.

I walked into the ring on a horse named Sundae and proceeded to have the three best trips of my life. I rode straight, I planned my track, I was nervous and somehow also in control, and I used my newfound knowledge of how to ride to execute a strategic course. I felt a world of possibility open up to me—there is rationality, formula, and meaningful hard work to put into a performance.

When I dismounted, I consciously remember thinking that I would never need lucky socks again. In the last seven years, I have had success in every helmet, every sock, every shirt, and with everything I have eaten for breakfast. I have ridden all over the country on horses that I know, horses that I do not know, horses that I was nervous on, and horses that I was more nervous on, and found success and positive rides and great jumps every time out.

Reflecting on my beginnings with Balmoral, I was so struck by how there was no blame—it was all learning. Traci is obsessed with learning. I was not told "if only" anything … if only I was stronger, if only I practiced more, if only I had someone else's body, if only I wasn't wearing my 20-year-old pull on boots—comments that had been made to me by many other people. At the ring, we got done what we could and saved the rest for a future lesson.

True educational experiences are about growth, which is so individual and can take so many forms. We need pathways to find our goals. When we know better, we can all do better, without diminishing our pasts. Reading this book, I hope you see things in your own barn and program to make permanent change for the betterment of your horses. As we grow, we all have more to offer our horses, our people, and our sport. We need our teachers to brighten the pathways to our goals, not push us toward darkness with shame.

Over the years, I have come to respect Traci and Carleton so much more as I see them work with people with all types of learning styles, goals, and previous experiences in this sport. They focus on my drive with the intention to bring out the best in me, someone who is a bit late and messy. Watching their program and the success inspires me to be more careful and more purposeful in every action, meeting my inherent self with aspirations of learning more and embracing other instincts.

 This book came from a place of wanting everyone in our sport to have a more positive experience and feel empowered to take on their equestrian career in a manner that makes sense for their own life. Our horses deserve the best we can come up with and give them. Our people deserve to be trained with respect and compassion. We all have different goals and constraints, but we can all proceed *With Purpose*. —*Piper*

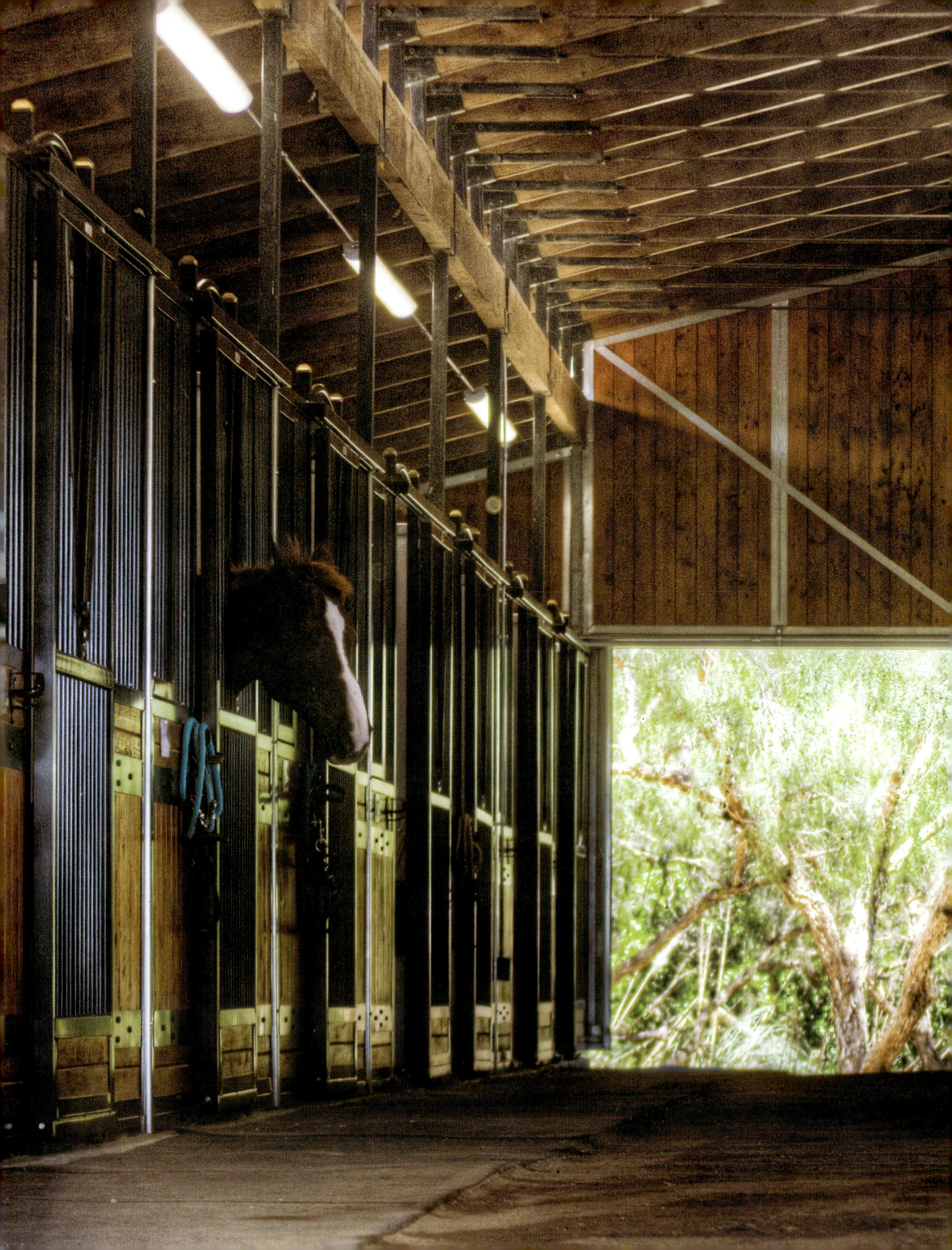

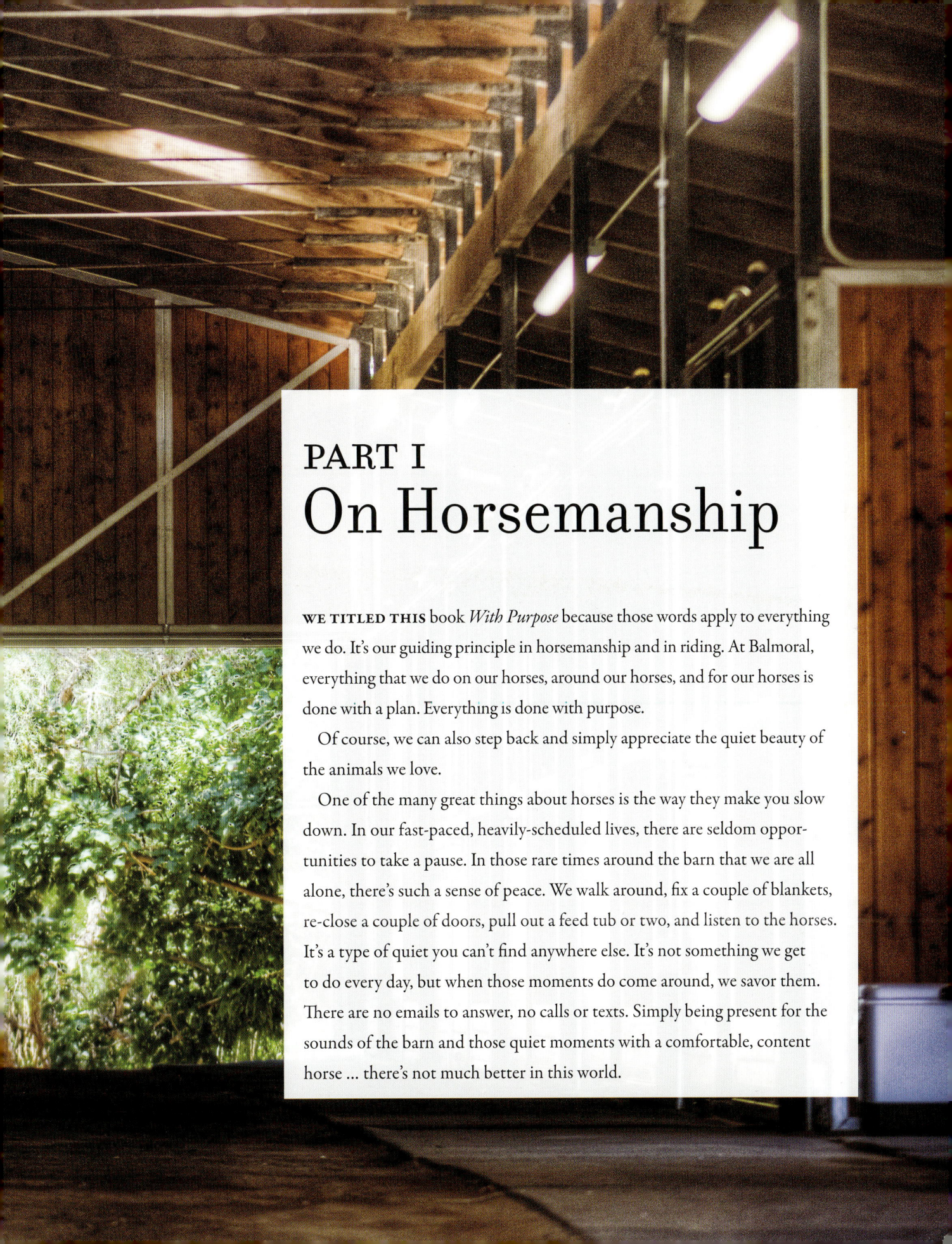

PART I
On Horsemanship

WE TITLED THIS book *With Purpose* because those words apply to everything we do. It's our guiding principle in horsemanship and in riding. At Balmoral, everything that we do on our horses, around our horses, and for our horses is done with a plan. Everything is done with purpose.

Of course, we can also step back and simply appreciate the quiet beauty of the animals we love.

One of the many great things about horses is the way they make you slow down. In our fast-paced, heavily-scheduled lives, there are seldom opportunities to take a pause. In those rare times around the barn that we are all alone, there's such a sense of peace. We walk around, fix a couple of blankets, re-close a couple of doors, pull out a feed tub or two, and listen to the horses. It's a type of quiet you can't find anywhere else. It's not something we get to do every day, but when those moments do come around, we savor them. There are no emails to answer, no calls or texts. Simply being present for the sounds of the barn and those quiet moments with a comfortable, content horse ... there's not much better in this world.

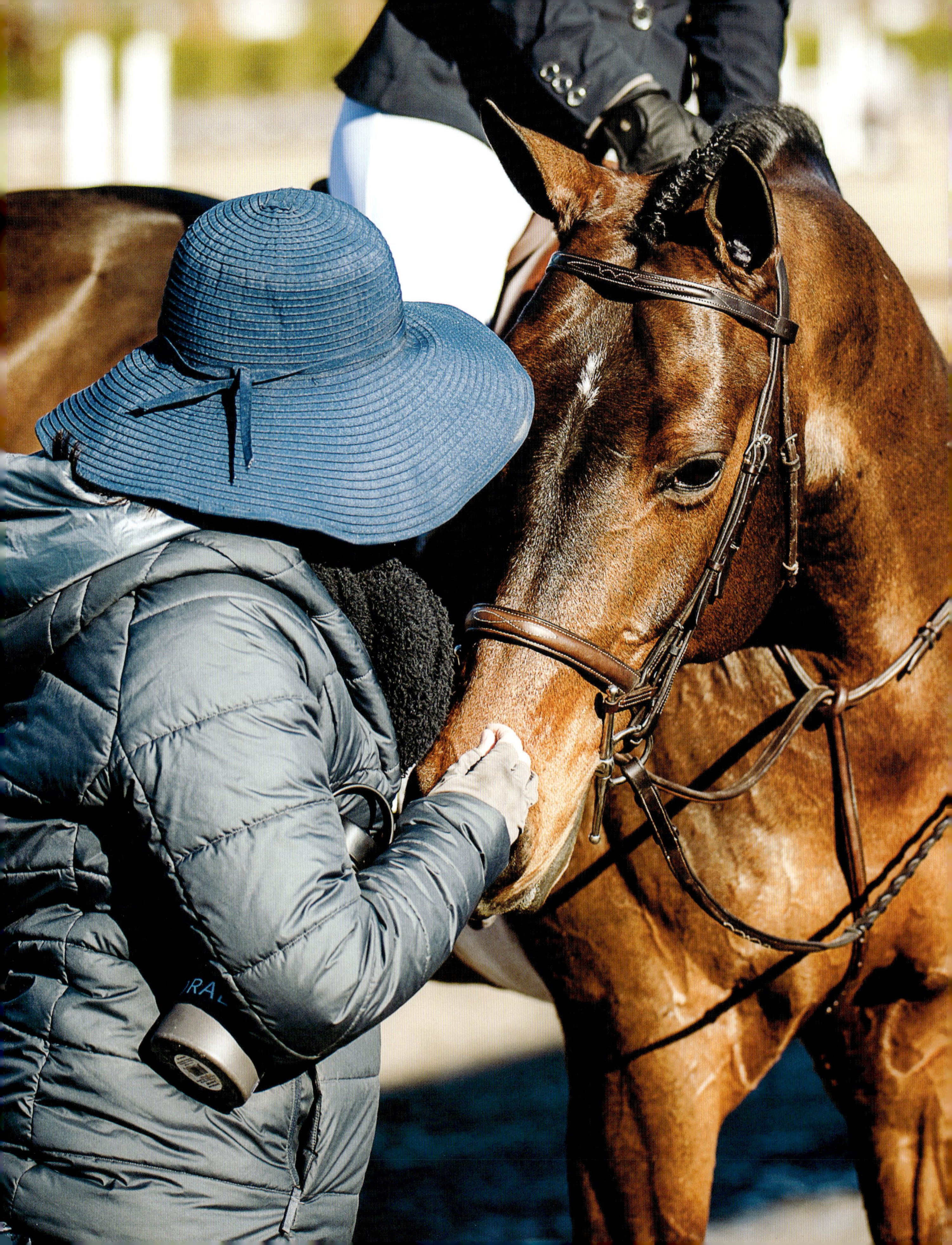

CHAPTER 1
The Horse Comes First

"THE HORSE COMES FIRST." It might be one of the most overused phrases in our industry, and for many people, it's just an empty promise. We hope to show you throughout this book how we act on this concept, day in and day out. More importantly, we hope to inspire you to do the same with your animals. Horses are always trying to tell us something. Our job is to do our best to listen and respond.

What would this feel like if I were the horse?

We ask ourselves this question dozens of times every day. To us, good horsemanship means watching our horses in every scenario and adjusting their environments, as well as our actions, to make them as comfortable as possible. It's not just about the riding. In fact, riding is only one little part of it. Our goal is to know our horses completely. We watch the horses in their stalls, we watch them jog, we watch them in turnout. That's our calling as horsemen, and we take it very seriously.

It's also worth noting that putting the horse first in every way will ultimately show up in the ring. Everything you do to take care of your animals will be reflected in how they perform. Anyone focused on the performance of their animal will greatly benefit from paying more attention to all the other areas of that horse's life.

Everyone starting out in our sport has at least one thing in common: We

> "Horsemanship transcends all disciplines." —CB

are captivated by horses. A fundamental love for the animal is the most basic prerequisite to riding. Where do people get lost along the way? We think it's the degree to which they value true horsemanship.

Look up "horsemanship" in the dictionary and you'll get a very different definition from ours. Merriam-Webster's first definition of "horseman" is "a rider or driver of horses." And the Oxford Learner's dictionary defines horsemanship as "skill in riding horses." Notice there's nothing about feeling the horse, knowing the horse, or dedicating yourself to the care of horses.

We believe true horsemen recognize that there's so much more to horsemanship than riding. And so, our own definition of horsemanship goes something like this: "Prioritizing the animal's needs and comfort and working to understand each individual horse from their own point of view in order to provide them with the best care and training possible."

As you'll read in the chapters that follow, we encourage caring for every horse based on their own specific and unique needs. There is simply no one-size-fits-all approach with animals.

> "The most important thing I can do is to encourage everyone in our industry to keep horsemanship alive. Challenge our younger, up-and-coming professionals to raise their standards. Encourage them to learn to see things from the horse's point of view. Be sensitive to the horses. Put the horses first, always. Teach the young professionals to treat their clients, employees, and fellow exhibitors with the utmost respect. One comment, one piece of encouragement, can make a difference. It can be the deciding factor for whether those who make up the next generation become good people and excellent horsemen." —CB
> (ADAPTED FROM HIS NATIONAL SHOW HUNTER HALL OF FAME ACCEPTANCE SPEECH)

CHAPTER 2

Care and Organization

CARING FOR YOUR animals is a significant part of horsemanship. And a big part of care is organization and cleanliness, so we will return to these concepts over and over. It's so important to keep everything clean and tidy—your horses, your equipment, and yourself.

As for organization, the way we do things at Balmoral involves a lot of lists and administration.

The office is a major part of horsemanship for us. If you prioritize individual care for all the horses in your program, you're going to have a whole lot of dates and notes to organize.

For instance, every time a horse gets shod, we update our shared server list with the horse's name, date they were shod, and any special notes. The same goes for the vet. Any time the horse receives a treatment, worming, vaccinations, or anything else, it all goes on the list. This helps us stay organized at home, but it's also essential for when we're at the horse show. This system allows us to pull up all the information on any horse right on our phones.

We also take photos of any new horse coming into the barn. We take them from the side, front, and back, along with photos of the horse's condition, their legs, their shoeing. We note anything like a big tendon, a scrape or a cut, and occasionally take videos of the horse jogging on a straight line, in case of any soundness issues. This way we have a visual record of everything on day one. It's helpful to have these things documented and it can also be fun to look back on those "intake" photos after the horse has been in our program for a while to track the fruits of our labor.

HORSE MAINTENANCE

Our administrative system, as explained above, is not the only way to do things, of course. But having a system—your system—for horse maintenance is essential.

There's a reason the phrase "no hoof, no horse" has persisted for so long. Shoeing is key to your horse's well-being. We don't just shoe our horses every five or six weeks. We make those decisions based on each individual horse. Some horses need to be shod every four weeks, and some horses go ten. Sometimes they might go even longer (if we're trying to get more foot to work with), but there's always a reason. Sometimes we just shoe one foot, or two or three. Each situation is unique. Is it easier to just put every horse in the barn on a six-week schedule? Yes. But managing horse care and maintenance with purpose means working on a horse-by-horse basis. This does require more work, but we find that it keeps our animals happier and more sound. It works, and it's worth it.

This philosophy extends to the horses' dental work, the chiropractor, and every other aspect of horse care. This way, we know that we've done everything we possibly can to keep each horse as healthy as it can be.

> "We never treat two horses the same. Every horse is an individual and we treat every horse as if it's the best horse we've ever had." —CB

TURNOUT

Every turnout situation is different, based largely on where you live. But the common goal for every horse should be providing opportunities for it to stretch its body and roll. Horses who live primarily in a stall will particularly benefit from moving and rolling in a turnout space. It's good for their bodies and loosens them up. Rolling is essential, just like bucking and galloping. Horses were made to roam and move. Turnout is beneficial to a horse's mental health, too.

As a function of geography, some horses have access to lots of turnout, some have less, and some have almost none at all. And while it's easy to issue a blanket statement about turnout and say "the more, the better," that's not always true.

For horses that show regularly, being turned out for twelve hours a day wouldn't necessarily be the best thing for them. Horses adapt to their environment and their routines, and while some horses are surely happier being outside as much as possible, others would just stand at the gate waiting for you. Therefore, the more productive question becomes: How can you best use the environment that you have to give your horse access to stretching and moving his body? They don't want to stand in a box twenty-three hours per day.

At one of our facilities in California, we have small turnout areas for the horses, but we also use our large outdoor ring for individual turnout opportunities. Moving the jumps to the center of the ring transforms it into a great turnout space. Sometimes, right after a ride, we'll untack a horse and let them run around and roll in the ring, enjoying a romp right after working. In many programs where turnout is limited, including ours, we also incorporate the treadmill to get the horses out and moving. But nothing can replace the way that rolling allows horses to stretch their bodies and play, so we strongly advise all horsemen to provide opportunities for their animals to do so.

Horses are roaming animals, so the more they can move, the better chance you have at maintaining their health. Show horses are used to being kept in stalls, so you have to get creative about finding ways for horses to move around beyond riding, like the use of a treadmill, European walker, or supervised turnout in a ring. Hills are great, too, so don't worry if your paddock isn't perfectly flat.

Each horse is an individual and every horse adapts to its environment. If horses are well cared for and happy, you can work with turnout limitations.

> "Do not get too carried away with natural horsemanship and natural environment. Horses adapt to their environment. Proper and thorough care is far more important." —CB

STALLS

It's easy to look at a stall, consider its dimensions and bedding, and call it a day. But there is so much more to think about when it comes to the comfort of your animal, both in their stall at home and at horse shows. There are plenty of adaptations you can make to maximize your horse's comfort and safety.

Start by taking note of the direction the barn faces. North, south, east, or west? Does it get morning sun or afternoon sun? Then, look at the overhang, and the way the air moves through the barn. When you look at the physicality of the individual stall, ask yourself, "Does it get a lot of light?" "Does the air move through it?" "Is the stall made of metal or wood?" Wood is ideal, while metal walls will feel colder. Plus, if the walls are metal, a horse that's lying down won't be able to get the traction they need to push off the wall, making them more likely to get cast (or stuck). We usually cover metal walls with wooden boards that extend about a third of the way up the wall, or we run a single board to provide traction and support as needed.

Next, you can look at the ground and ask, "What is the construction of the flooring?" If you've got rubber mats, what's underneath them? Is there a drain in the stall? Those are important considerations so that the floor of the stall doesn't hold too much moisture, which can cause problems with thrush and the horses' feet not growing properly.

Ask yourself whether a barn's fly system is effective. What sort of products are involved? At Balmoral, we like to stay away from potential toxins as much as possible and find that fly systems, as a whole, aren't always great solutions. We mostly use fans to keep flies at bay. And flies do serve a purpose: When the horses go after them, it keeps the horses moving, turning, and stretching. So, we don't view flies as a nuisance to completely eliminate. Cleaning stalls regularly often helps alleviate fly issues as well.

Both at home and at the Desert International Horse Park, where we show all winter, we've modified the stalls to add kickboards in the entryway. Horses have to step over them to come in and out of the stall, which actually benefits them because it's like a mini exercise—they have to use their brain to keep track of where their feet are each time they enter and exit their stall. Also, the addition of that simple board keeps the shavings inside the stalls. We use decomposed granite (DG) as the stall base (for drainage and for the horse's comfort) with rubber mats on top, and then the shavings on top of that. We bank the shavings along the walls so the horses are less likely to get cast when they lie down at night.

We also add mangers to all of our stalls, setting off a corner of each stall as the designated place for that horse's hay. We do this for a few reasons. First and foremost, it keeps the horse's head down while they eat, which is best for their bodies since it's their natural grazing position.

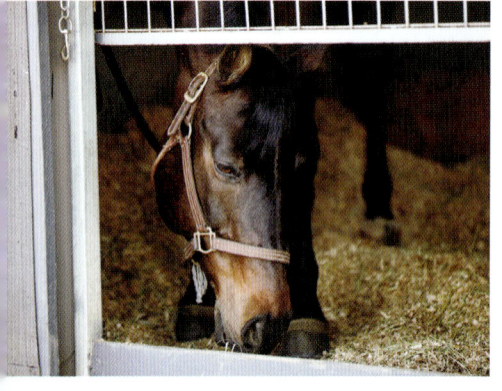

> "In the old days, people used to build stone barns. I went to a barn in Ohio and I noticed the stones inside the barn were jagged but the stones on the outside of the barn were smooth. I thought, 'That is so weird. Why did they not do it the other way?' Then I realized they intentionally did that so the horse could create leverage and traction to push away from the stall wall to get up. In barns, as in horses, form follows function." —CB

As horses are grazing animals, we like to keep food in front of them at all times. While grazing, the horse brings their hind end up underneath them and picks their back up. And that positioning, which is what we're trying to create when we ride, becomes more natural over time because the horses are muscled up from eating that way all day long. We don't believe in using hanging hay nets in the stalls. Unlike eating hay from the ground, eating out of hay nets over time can cause a horse to become more inverted. Also, while eating from the ground, the horse is using its jaw and moving its tongue, which is what you want when they're in the bridle.

The second reason we recommend the use of a manger in the corner of the stall is that it keeps the hay in one spot. The horse isn't dragging it around in their stall, so there's less hay wasted and less clean-up. If you choose to go the manger route with your own stalls, we recommend moving the horses between stalls periodically. Depending upon the corner in which the manger is placed, the horse will naturally have one leg forward of the other. And you don't want them eating for hours a day in only that one position, as it will lead to imbalance in their bodies and their musculature and make them one-sided.

Each of our stalls has a Himalayan salt block, and often a mineral block (in addition to the electrolytes we give them in their food), because we want to be sure we keep the horses drinking.

Since the weather can vary so greatly where we live and show, every stall also has a fan and we loosely tie the horse's blanket in the corner with a piece of cotton rope. We don't recommend hanging blankets on the outside of the stall because they get dirty and dusty, and the horses tend to reach around and grab them. Plus, the blankets look messy on the outside. When they're folded neatly in a corner—buckles and straps to the inside—the horses tend to leave them alone. As far as a horse is concerned, the folded blanket just becomes part of the stall. To mitigate any remaining risk from having the blankets inside, we use a soft cotton rope to tie the blanket into the corner because the rope would break if the horse were to get hung up in it.

We use stall gates with yokes so that the horses can see out and have more airflow. We also have a technique with the stall gates that's proved to be very useful. On each of our stall gates (which act as the stall door), we add a bungee cord. This way we don't have to clip the stall shut each time—the door automatically stays closed. If we are getting a horse in or out of the stall, we take the bungee off on one end so the gate can open freely. When the horse is inside the stall, we put the bungee back on tightly, with the hook facing out so the horse cannot catch his nose or eye on it. This is a way to keep things efficient and so you don't have to keep latching the gate when going in and out multiple times a day.

You also want your horse's stall to feel as open as possible. Other than rare exceptions, it's better for a horse to be able to stick its head out. We choose the stall gates with the yokes so the horses cannot get their heads around to chew on things. But they can still see out and the stall feels bigger, lighter, and more airy.

CB giving Sundae a quick drink of water by hand at the horse show.

WATERING

At Balmoral, we water our horses with hoses and buckets. Always. Getting horses drinking and keeping them drinking is a huge part of their overall well-being. We hang two or three buckets in each stall. And some horses prefer drinking from the ground from metal tubs. Automatic watering systems are all turned off or removed at our facilities. We find that you cannot easily monitor how much your horse is drinking if their water is automatically being filled. It's also harder to clean an automatic system, whereas you can just dump a bucket and wash it out. We aren't claiming to have the only "right" way to do things with this decision (or any decisions!), but it's part of our system and we believe in it.

In our experience, horses also typically drink less from an automatic watering system than they do from buckets. Horses are innately claustrophobic. When

> "One time we had a mare who was not drinking. I was driving one of the tractor trailers and I stopped at a truck stop that had apples. I got the squishiest apple, squished it in my hand, and fed it to the horse. When a horse eats an apple, they will usually drink next. If you ever watch a horse after feeding them an apple, they get syrupy around their lips and they will go drink to try to wash off their mouth. So what did this mare do? She started drinking. All it took was an apple." —CB

they have to put their face down into a waterer, they may drink less at a time. Automatic watering systems also make noise, which can scare the horses. So, they dip in and then lift their nose back out. But if you watch a horse at a water trough or pond, they keep their nose in there. Now, they may not be drinking the whole time, but they feel comfortable keeping their nose inside. The wider the bucket or the drinking vessel is, the more a horse will drink. If a horse's eye level is right at the top of the bucket, or in an open trough, they will drink more. That is their flight instinct at work. They have to be able to see, so they are not going to put their head inside past their eye.

We have a big metal water tub filled with water and carrots outside our barns at home and at the show. The horses will look for it after working, dig for carrots, and drink the water before they go to get untacked. It might be a good twenty to thirty minutes before they get to their stalls if they're drinking, eating carrots, and taking their time. We never rush home. (More on this in chapter 12!)

We've also found that a lot of horses won't drink on a truck, and you have to teach them to do so. One way to do this is to bring the buckets from their stalls and put them in the truck without cleaning them. Water tastes different in different buckets, so when you provide horses with their own buckets, they will usually drink more.

GROOMING AND COMFORT

One of the first things we do when we see our horses in the morning is to clean out the corners of their eyes. You know how they can get kind of crusty or goopy in there? Horses can't fix that for themselves. So it's become a habit for us around the barn.

As for grooming horses, every situation is different. People who keep their horses at home are fully responsible for the grooming of their animals. If you board your horse, each barn has their own way of doing things. Some run largely on a system of self-care, in which the clients are the ones grooming their horses. You've got full service barns, where any number of professional grooms are in charge of the horses' care. And then you've got everything in between, with many boarding barns offering services like grooming and tacking to their clients.

We believe that no matter your barn's specific situation or offerings, at the bare minimum, every horse person should know the basics of grooming. You should know how to pick out your horse's feet (always the first step, so that if a shoe is loose or missing, you can alert your barn manager or trainer), and

> "I am adamant about good grooming. You need to curry horses, you need to rub on them. It brings out the oil in their coat. We try not to give a lot of baths, not to use a lot of water. And grooming needs to be a relaxed experience for the horse. It needs to make them feel good." —TB

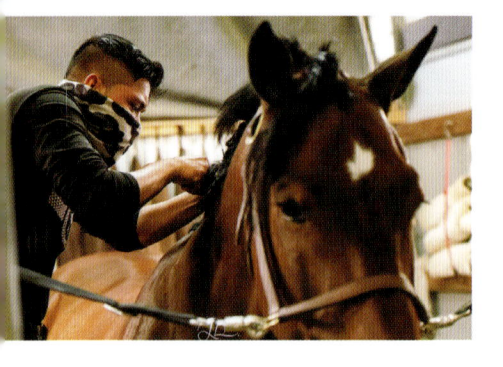

how to curry and brush your horse. When you know your horse physically, you can observe any changes. Does that ankle always get puffy? Is it hot? Was that bump always there? Is the horse cranky about the saddle?

Also try to be mindful of the routines involved in grooming your horse or pony. For example, in one of our barns, the grooms would always lead the horse from the left and then turn them to the left to put them in the cross ties. But our cross ties have open space in both the front and the back, so we asked the grooms to think about these movements. Why make the horse spin in a small circle when you could walk them through the back and then attach the cross ties without having to turn around? If you were a horse, would you want to spin in a small circle or walk in through the back without making a tight turn?

Questions like these are also good to think about if you are building a barn. It seems like a small detail, but if your animal has to turn in a tight circle to the left every day, five or six days a week, that will ultimately take a toll. If you've got space to do things in a different way in order to make the horses more comfortable, do it. Mix it up. Turn to the right sometimes!

It comes back to one of the things we say on a daily basis: "Be the horse." What would be the more comfortable maneuver if you were the horse?

Here's another example of how to consider the animal's comfort and make changes accordingly. We had a pony from Germany who was breaking the cross ties while getting a bath. We had to think about what the pony was used to from his former home—probably having a wall behind him in the wash stall. It's not the horse's fault (it never is!) and most often, misbehavior means the animal is trying to tell you something. In the case of the broken wash stall cross ties, the pony was telling us, "I do not like that. I feel insecure without something behind me." Most horses feel this way.

There are so many things that are going to happen with horses that are not within our control. It's just like riding—always control what you can.

So, in the case of this pony, we paired one of our grooms with him in order to learn more about the pony's likes and dislikes, build his trust, and figure out solutions to make him more comfortable. When we had the pony on the cross ties for grooming and tacking, we would be sure to use the cross ties that had a back behind them to make the pony feel secure. But the wash stall at one of our properties doesn't have a back, so we would either put up a board or have someone stand with the pony without tying him. It was just about giving this pony a little extra attention until he felt more at ease.

Even when it comes to basic grooming, knowing your horse will make for a more comfortable and enjoyable experience (for both of you!). Some horses are more thin-skinned and do not like a stiff brush. You learn these things by being hands-on with your particular animal.

Like any athlete, your horse needs to stay warm in cooler temperatures.

> "I am always cold. So, if I have a 7:00 a.m. lesson and I see the guys with down coats on and a body-clipped horse standing in the cross ties with nothing on, I think, 'You just took that horse out of their stall, and now they're standing here naked and we are going to let the rider go ride them and expect them to behave?' As soon as you take the blankets off, that horse needs to be covered. They are athletes. Your athlete needs to stay warm!" —TB

It's also important to "be the horse" when it comes to decisions around body clipping and exposing your horse to the elements.

We have heaters in our cross ties and once we pull the blankets off, we put a cooler on the horse while we're getting them ready. When we're grooming the front end, we pull the cooler back. While we're grooming the back end, we flip the cooler forward so the horse is never too cold.

We also use quarter sheets a lot at home, particularly for the body-clipped horses in the winter and on early morning rides. If you have a horse that tends to be a little stiff or tight, it's all the more important to keep their muscles warm and pliable. With a little repetition, most horses get used to quarter sheets. Another added benefit is it helps the horse get used to having something added into the mix while you're riding. If you've desensitized them a little bit with a quarter sheet, it can be easier to introduce new things for showing, like a fake tail or a shadbelly on the rider.

If your horse isn't accustomed to wearing a quarter sheet and you're concerned about how they might react, you can lunge them in it for a few minutes before getting on. Consider the different types of quarter sheets, too. Some have a band that goes under the tail and some don't. Some hook to the girth and some don't. The materials are important, too. The polar fleece quarter sheets tend to be more lightweight and are more likely to flap around in the breeze. The lined, heavier wool quarter sheets won't flap as much.

We also have a rule that we do not touch the horse's tails. We barely brush them! This will preserve as much tail as humanly possible for you when it is time to show. There's an old Saddlebred method where they put some baby oil or ShowSheen in the clean tail and then loosely braid it with a piece of soft cotton flannel, leaving some hair out to swish flies. We do that sometimes. This way we aren't constantly brushing it and pulling the hair out. (You'll be amazed at how long and full the tail is when you take the braid out. Just remember to do so monthly and then wash and condition the tail.

Then start over with a new clean piece of flannel.)

All these little things add up to create the end result of your horse's condition and turnout.

TREATS

Some people love to feed their horses treats all the time. This is obviously a personal choice, but we feel it's important to note that feeding treats in a regular manner is something you do for you. It's not for the horse, and it can lead to biting problems, mouthing, and lack of discipline and respect in the cross ties (which is why we prohibit treats in that particular spot). For clients who want to give their horses treats, we ask that they put them in the horse's feed bucket or on the ground in the stall only.

Horse people are generally also dog people, so it's only natural that they may want to feed horses treats the same way they do with dogs. But horses just don't respond to food rewards in the same way as dogs. We do put carrots in the horses' feed, and we use treats to teach a horse to bend, flex, or to work on building trust. We just try to be careful about too much hand-feeding and recommend that others do the same.

Our rule about hand-feeding treats can be really hard for the kids (and adults!), who often want to give their animals a reward. We explain to them that when you feed treats in the cross ties, the other horses are going to get wound up, which is not kind to them, nor to the staff who work for us. We also

> "Many Grand Prix riders like to keep a small treat in their pocket to reward their horse for its work immediately after a ride. For us, it's just more about not giving treats all the time, particularly in the cross ties." —CB

> "What is good care? It is different for every horse." —TB

talk about why they want to treat the horse (as a reward) and offer alternatives. We believe that attention and affection are just as good rewards for horses. Better, really, because of the negative behaviors that often result from too much hand-feeding. We show our riders how to stroke a horse's neck or rub on their withers, which horses often prefer to actual patting (which would feel better to you?), and encourage the kids to spend time with their animal on the ground.

Adults also want to reward their horses and know that their horses are content, which is totally understandable. Horses know if you are happy to see them, and that is the environment we encourage people to create. Dr. Charlie Boles, one of our vets, used to come to our barn in the city and say, "I can't believe it, but horses are so relaxed and happy here." We think that is because the people who work for us are happy to do their jobs, and the horses have a routine that makes them comfortable. We try really hard to understand our horses and to be relaxed around them and we think they can feel that. When you walk through a barn and you get that feeling of just wanting to take a deep breath, that barn is doing something right. That serves as a reward for a horse—you do not have to reward them with food.

CHAPTER 3
Think Like a Horse

NO ONE *REALLY* KNOWS what horses are thinking. If we did, it would make our jobs a whole lot easier. However, after several decades of working with horses, based on our experience and how horses react to us, we have some pretty good ideas.

Many a horseman has wondered what makes a performance horse happy, and from what we can tell, having a routine is paramount. And with a routine comes expectations. A show horse—and any horse, really, that has a job working with humans—has expectations placed on them. Understanding those expectations and knowing what's coming throughout their day seems to go a long way with a horse. Changing the routine can be jarring, and mixed messages about our expectations are confusing. So, to the best of our ability, we maintain a consistent routine and try to "speak horse" so the animals know what to expect.

Horses don't like surprises. Most of them don't like things happening too fast. Positive energy and feedback are important. So is physical comfort—the horse's body should feel good. If you're walking around and your knees hurt or your back hurts, you're not going to feel like you can perform at your best. We try to read the horses and take care of their physical comfort.

As previously mentioned, we aren't big on treats in our barns, but we understand that humans want to know how to best reward their horse for a job well

> "Our motto is routine, structure, expectation, positivity." —TB

> "You'll notice I never pet a horse. I stroke them. If you're going to tap a horse with a stick, isn't a hard pat the same thing? If you rub your horse, it's comforting. Think about how a pat versus a rub would feel to you." —CB

done. Horses work hard for us and expect nothing in return, so it's human nature to want to acknowledge their efforts. To reward them, we suggest focusing on attention and positive reinforcement.

We believe that if a horse thinks you are part of his herd, he will go along with you. There is a survival instinct at play, too—some horses might translate doing their job into getting fed. A lot of horses are very motivated by the reward that comes with doing their job, even if that reward is as simple as getting hay and water, kindness and attention.

Some horses enjoy their jobs more than others. People tend to say things like "that one loves its job," or "this horse loves to be at a show." How much truth is there to that? We believe that horses are individuals and should be treated as such.

We have one horse who is over twenty years old, and if you retired him and put him in a field, he would not do well. He needs to have a job and he needs to get brushed every day. Even if someone just takes him out, grooms him, gives him affection, and jumps a few jumps now and then, he is happy.

Horses like him need the interaction because that is all they know. Each horse is an individual as much as humans are. Some simply want to work more than others. Show horses are so domesticated that many lose a lot of their wildness and flight instinct, so what they're left with is their job and the human interaction that comes with it.

You can tell when show horses are eager to perform. We have a few who are a little blah about being ridden on the flat, but then you point them at the jumps and they become so much more engaged. It's all about the individual personalities and we try to work that into each horse's care and training program.

When something is important to you, the human, the horses can feel the difference. And when they go someplace new, or someplace really different from what they're used to, like Indoors,

"When my junior hunter got older and stopped horse showing, I could not turn her out. She would walk maybe fifteen feet away to graze, but she did not know anything but me and I had spent so much time with her. So, we ended up making her a school horse. One year, we didn't know that she was in foal. She never stopped teaching lessons, and two weeks after having the baby, she was teaching lessons again. She loved it. We tried to leave her just with the foal but she would stand by the gate and stare at the ring. So we finally put her in a pen with her foal and she did not ever mind leaving to teach a lesson or two. She gave us this look that said, 'I am good to go.' Some of these horses, that is just what they know." —CB

Allow your horse to go through the process of observing (so long as the behavior doesn't escalate).

it's an entirely new routine. They are getting all this attention and you are feeling intense, so they're going to feel that. They can feel when it's important. Special horses rise to the occasion.

SPEAKING HORSE

Horses perform at their best when they feel content, comfortable, and safe. As such, we are constantly assessing, to the best of our ability, what their behavior and body language are telling us. We think when the vibe of the entire team is relaxed, confident, and happy, the horses feel that and follow suit. If the atmosphere is tense, the horses pick up on that, too.

There are lots of ways to create a relaxed, confident, and happy atmosphere in your stable. Some people play music in their stable to create that type of atmosphere. But it mainly comes down to the people who work there, and the attitudes they bring with them. The horses will generally read that and react to it or mirror it.

There are subtle but translatable behaviors you can watch for, like when a horse opens their nostrils wide, sometimes paired with lifting their head and holding their breath. That means they're sensing something in the distance. It could be from an observational viewpoint or a defensive viewpoint. Horses are flight animals, so if they think there's something in the distance, they will raise their head slightly and open their nostrils to allow their senses to work. That doesn't mean there's anything wrong. But many people grab their horse or worry about a spook coming, instead of just allowing the process to happen. Try not to be (over) reactive. Sometimes you've got to let a horse go through the process. They do it all day long and most people don't notice. You may get on in the warmup ring and your horse looks down to the next warmup ring, raising his head and opening his nostrils, because there's a horse down there panicked by something. Your horse might observe that, and the best thing you can do is let them go through that process while you act as if you're relaxed (even if you're not). Do not let it escalate.

Another behavior that people tend to notice is yawning. It's a way for horses to relieve their muscles, first off, just like when we yawn. In fact, yawning is really an exaggeration of taking a deep breath. It's a sign of being relaxed. Think of this as a positive!

When a horse cocks their ear back, (possibly with their eye looking behind them), they're listening to you.

There are behaviors with the horse's tail that you can interpret as well. The underside of the tail is a very sensitive part of the horse's body. Clamping the tail down indicates distress or anger. If a horse swishes his tail in a relaxed manner, that means his body is loose and he's willing to do something. At times, the tail will also move as you close your leg—toward the side where you are adding pressure. A horse uses his tail for balance, so a fair amount of movement is to be expected. But lots of swishing of the tail can indicate a clashing of aids, or a form of discomfort or annoyance.

> "I have always taken pride in listening to the horse and treating each horse as an individual, and I remember them all for their unique traits that led them to become such stars in the show ring." —CB

> "When I hang out with the horses I sometimes let them breathe on me (they like our necks!) and I put my nose by theirs and breathe into their nostrils. And when they breathe back, you can feel them relax. We also like to rub a horse near the withers because that's where horses nuzzle each other." —TB

A lot of interpreting horse behaviors comes down to intuition. You have to be 100 percent present to really feel what your horse is feeling. And always putting yourself in your horse's shoes.

People ask us all the time, "How do you learn to speak horse?" "How do you know what's about to happen?" If you're paying attention and trying to understand the animals—and you're truly focused and not distracted or on your phone—you pick up on this stuff over time. You won't always be right, but you start to get the idea of what horses are trying to tell you. A lot of times, it's simply imagining what something feels like to a horse in order to "speak" their language, putting yourself in their position, and "being" the horse.

In another example, we had one horse that was coughing a bit and we put him on cough medicine and tried wetting his hay. We thought maybe it was allergies. Then we tried making the noseband really loose, so that horse could

> "We had a horse on trial for an adult, and we didn't know the horse very well. I was holding the horse for the rider at the mounting block, and I could just feel that the horse was anxious. I could feel him holding his breath and getting a little tense. As the rider swung her leg over, I could feel that the horse wasn't relaxed and it had some pent-up energy. The rider had only walked a little loop, and I told her to get off. She was confused, but she did. (Riders have to listen to their trainers, immediately and without question, to stay safe. Hesitation can be dangerous.) We took the horse over to the turnout and I told the rider I thought the horse needed to buck. We turned him out and he ran around, bucked three or four times, and came walking over to us as if to say, 'I'm done, thank you. Now we can proceed.' The rider got back on and the horse was perfect. The horse wasn't being bad before, he just needed to get some extra energy out. It was a cool Tuesday morning and the horse just needed a moment. We gave him a moment and then he was fine." —TB

> "Horses are always trying to tell us something. Our job is to always be listening and trying to understand them." —TB

open its mouth a little more and move his tongue—allowing him to swallow and breathe. And that was when he stopped coughing. It's all about putting yourself in that horse's position.

Your horse is also in tune to your breathing. This is another place to act as if you're relaxed, even if you're not. When you hold your breath, so does your horse. When your breath is shallow, your horse's is too. When we hear a horse take a deep breath, we automatically relax and feel grateful to know that the horse has relaxed, too. They have to be relaxed to perform their best. To us, that is a sign of a happy and content horse, whether you are riding or just working in the barn. A deep breath from a horse tells you that they

> "I try to sense what the horse is feeling and put myself in their situation so I can feel it." —CB

are comfortable and understand what is being asked of them. It's not that different from people!

If you want your horse to take a deep breath, remember that they will often mimic you. So if you take a deep breath in and then let it all out slowly, know that your horse will also relax. We use this on course and we build it into our course plan—where will we take a breath? After jump four? If you do a big, slow exhale on course, be ready to back it up with some leg because a lot of times the horses will almost stop! To them, it may feel like you're at the end of your course or exercise, and you're about to relax into a walk—but instead you want them to continue on after that moment of relaxation. It's a reset. A pause. Use it as a tool.

Oftentimes with novice or less experienced riders, we teach them to slow or stop their horses only from adjusting their breath (along with their weight). No other aids. They are always in awe when they feel how well it works!

It's always nice to see when a horse wants to be around you. We don't ever want our horses to be afraid of us. We try to win them over. Once we do, being with us is the horse's comfort. When a horse follows you, that's a great sign that he trusts you in his space.

CHAPTER 4
Establishing the Horse-Rider Relationship

HORSES ALWAYS SEEM to love certain people. What qualities do those people have? We think that horses feel a person's sincerity and their energy. Dogs and kids are the same way. Animals in general are just drawn to some people—they can tell that you love them. They're also looking to be around people from whom there are no surprises. Animals are attracted to people who are on their side, on their team. They get that. Horses can sense your energy even when you walk by their stalls—their senses are so much more acute than ours.

Certain people's energy is threatening to horses, while other people's energy is calming to them. And they can really sense fear. If you're afraid of them, they start to fear you—not like you're going to hurt them, but they fear that you're not going to be there for them, or that you're unpredictable. This goes back to a horse's flight instinct. If you're unpredictable, you're a predator, and then the flight instinct kicks in. If you're unpredictable, you're the enemy, and to a horse, that trans-

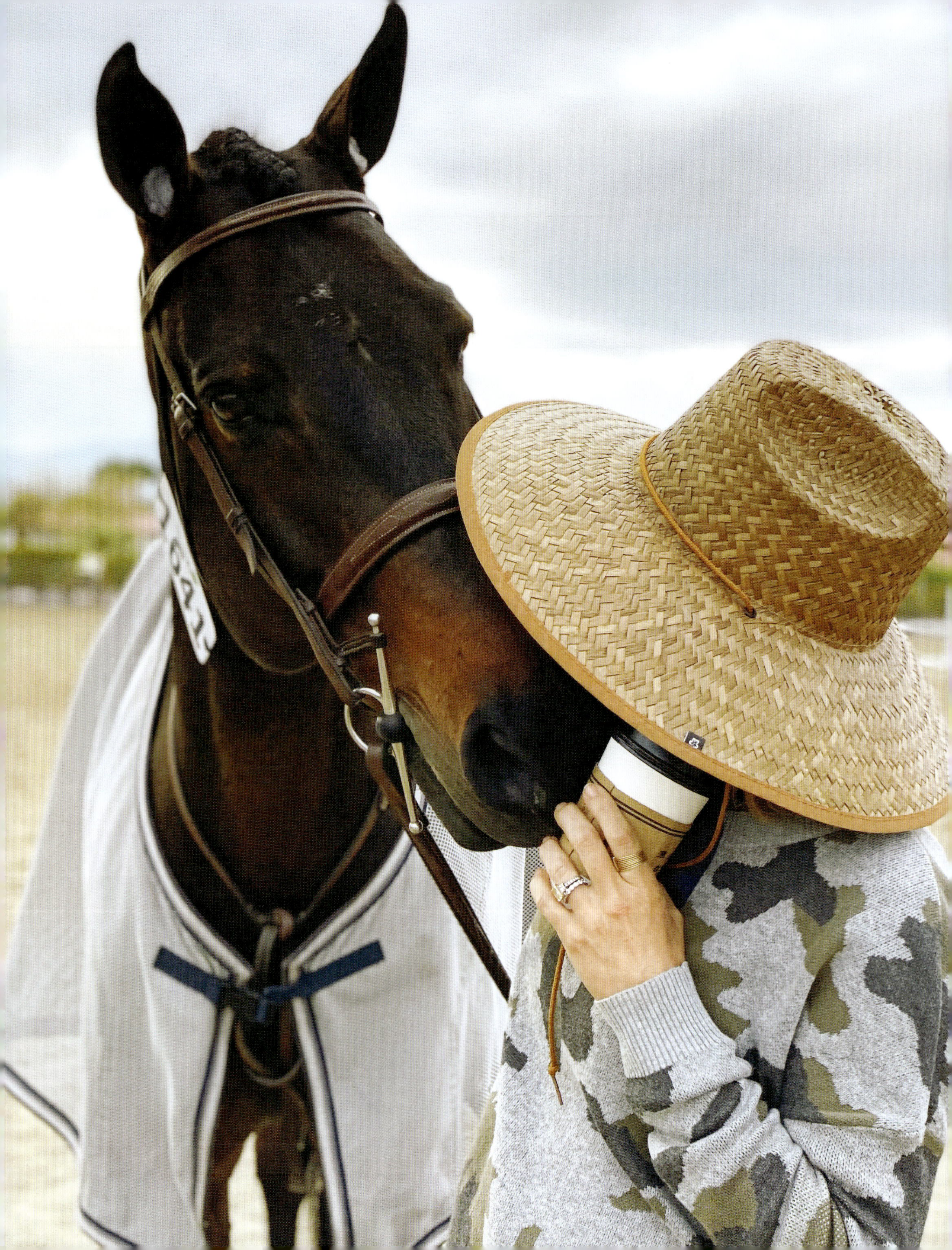
641

lates into "I might have to run away."

The energy that horses pick up from you is a lot like when you smile at someone, or even if you just smile with your eyes. Horses, like people, can feel that. It's a visceral thing. And if you're the type of person a horse wants to be around, you're likely to also be the type of person who can read and understand horses.

An interesting method for working with a horse who's felt threatened before is to lower yourself below them—literally crouch down—and then slowly bring yourself up to their level. The way you're breathing is also important with this type of horse. If you walk up to them and you're holding your breath, that's going to put the horse off and make them nervous. So even if you're a little nervous around the horse, you have to act as if you're feeling extra zen. It's about

> "It sometimes takes a year to fully develop a partnership with a horse. It's just like a human relationship. There are little intricacies of getting to know each other—what you like, what you don't like, what makes you happy, what makes you anxious. Just getting to know a horse by seeing the look in their eye is sometimes all it takes. Learning what they like as far as preparation. When each one is having a good day and a bad day, how does that play out? Do you feed off of each other positively or negatively? Do you push each other's buttons and how do you work that out? Do you pick a fight or walk away? When do you push it? It's a lot to learn and digest. There has to be a give and take and you have to treat it like a relationship. It is a partnership. Everyone, at the end of the day, needs to get their needs met to some degree." —TB

creating that atmosphere for the horse so they feel comfortable and relaxed.

We have a rider who leases a slightly anxious horse of ours. This rider comes six days a week and she grooms the horse for an hour, she gets on, she works him for half an hour, she gets off. She grooms him again. And in the six months that she's been leasing him, he's turned into a different horse. He's gotten fat and put on muscle because he's happy and relaxed. This horse probably never had his own person before. But because his rider has a routine with him and the horse trusts her, she's his person. You see that in certain horses. The time that people take with them makes all the difference. The connection is real. This horse in particular, if his person is on the property, you can see that he's looking for her.

Great horseman Jimmy Lee said to us, "Treat every horse like he's the best horse you've ever had." And we believe this. If you treat a horse like he's the best horse you've ever had, you're going to work to bring out the best in him. You're going to show respect to that horse. And you're going to look at what he can do with his positives, and bring those positives out. Your horse will blossom.

If a horse has someone who cares about him and treats him like the best horse, that will impact the horse's confidence too. Horses don't know how much they cost. If you think the horse can do something, and the horse thinks he can do it, he is going to perform better and try harder. There's always an exception to the rule, but usually, horses will try to do whatever you're asking. The majority will follow your lead. Some people don't put the effort into treating each horse like the best horse they ever had. But when you do, the results can be magical.

CHAPTER 5
Conformation

PART OF BEING a good horseman is knowing what makes a well-built equine athlete who will perform in an ideal manner. In this chapter, we'll walk you through what it means for a horse to have good conformation and how it's imperative to performance and soundness.

From a historical perspective, conformation has always been integral because you had to have a horse that was durable and would last. Historically, when people are breeding horses, they are trying to breed athletes, whether it is a racehorse or a jumping horse, so they are breeding for correctness. Form is function, so a horse is going to hold up better if their body is more correct.

To put it in simple terms, you can use the analogy of a table. If your table has one leg that's not straight, it is not going to be sturdy. When you stand your horse up, you want to have four corners to your table. If the horse is standing a little out behind itself, your "table" is going to lean forward. That's a very basic way to start to understand conformation.

Overall, a horse has to have athletic balance—that's a must. They should have a long neck, a wither, and a distinguished hip. Their hip shouldn't slope off behind, it should have a little plateau. The way their legs line up underneath their body is very important. They can't have a narrow base or a wide, tight shoulder. They have to have an athletic, fluid shoulder down the leg to the base of the foot, and the foot and the pastern should have the same angle. The feet should match.

CB's Notes on Conformation . . .

Our former conformation hunter, Pritchard Hill (now owned by the Lignelli family) has stature and presence. He looks like an athlete. He gives you that athletic presence. Others have stature and they're correct, but they don't give you the presence that they can dominate. This one is regal in how he carries himself and how he's put together. There are no flaws in this picture. He's as good as we've seen in decades.

STRAIGHTNESS OF THE HIND END
The old saying was that the hind lower leg should be like a fence post: Straight off the rump from the hock down. The hock should have angulation to it. If you have to give somewhere, I'd rather have the hock come underneath; the hock should never be out behind the horse. That's called "camped out" and it means it would be very difficult for the horse to bring his hind end up to propel.

ANGLE AND LENGTH OF THE PASTERNS
The angle and length of the pastern in front should be similar to the angle or slope of the shoulder. If the horse were a painting, it would be like one hill in front of another. The hind pasterns should have a bit less angle than the front. It's a concern when the hind pastern has more angle than the front.

FEET
You have to have a heel and a cupped sole. Even though the judge can't see the sole, those feet need to be very similar and symmetrical. A good, healthy, strong foot. "No foot, no horse."

PROPORTIONS
The neck should be longer than the middle of the horse, and the middle should be longer than the hind quarters. If you think about the proportions in relation to each other, the neck would be 3 ⅛, the middle 2 ¾, and the hindquarters 2 ¼.

EXPRESSION
The expression is very important, as is the placement of the eyes. When judging hunters, the first thing you see as a judge when they enter the ring is their head. Also, the eyes need to be set wide in front, and you want a horse with a large eye. Old horsemen always used to say the wider the forehead in proportion to their body, the smarter they were.

ANGLE OF THE SHOULDER
I've never seen a horse with too much. I've seen a lot of horses with not enough. The shoulder has to have a slope to it that's gradual and fluid. When you look at the horse, it should be like a painting that is all fluid. There's no specific percentage or number when you're considering the angle of the shoulder. The shoulder angle has to do with the elasticity, which creates range of motion. You have to have a shoulder that's put on symmetrically to the rest of their body. Otherwise the horse will move wide. Or if the front legs are too close together, they move narrow and will have difficulty getting the front end out of the way. A horse should have a wide enough chest to put his head down between his front legs and graze.

When we are thinking about buying a horse, we often look at each other and go, "Do you think it could model?" That's our way of asking: How is the function going to follow the form? The answer to the model question doesn't always have to be yes. Every horse isn't going to be a model winner. But when we saw Pritchard Hill, for example, we thought he could model. He didn't have any obvious flaws. He was correct. His legs were straight, no blemishes, no bumps or bruises. His neck was long, his back was short, and he had nice angles to his shoulder and hips. He had good feet, good expression, a good hind end. So he definitely checked all the boxes.

There are also the intangible elements of conformation: The horse's expression, and just the feeling. You can check all the boxes and the horse still might not have great presence, or they might not have any swagger in their walk or any swing in their shoulder.

SHOWING IN A MODEL CLASS

When you watch people lead their horse into the model class, do they walk in with purpose? Does their horse walk with purpose? If the horse walks in leaning on the front end, even if it's a pretty horse, it won't give you that feeling and excitement.

Another element that's hard to quantify when you're looking at confor-

> "The conformation division requires conditioning and soundness in great detail. When I judge a conformation model class, I always stand back and look at the horses as a group. You'd be amazed which ones stand out more that way. The best horsemen I've seen look at the horse's balance. They look at the horse's alertness and demeanor. And the horse has to walk. It's not specified in the model, but a horse must have a busy, forward swagger to their walk or they're not going to be able to carry their weight across the ground." —CB

mation is the way the horse stands across the ground. It's a little bit like a football player that takes up a lot of surface area across the ground. But the horse also has to be able to do ballet, so to speak.

Showing a horse or pony in a model class also goes back to the basics, like the care and feeding. We always say: Control what you can control. That's part of the presentation. You can control how you condition your horse. You control the bridle you put on, and how it fits. If your horse has a conformation flaw, you can still think about how to best present that horse to minimize the shortcoming. If your horse has a shorter neck, maybe you skip having a bridle path and put in an extra few braids.

A good habit to instill at home if you're ever going to model your horse or pony is to stroke them on the neck and not on the face. If you're always messing with your horse's face, your horse is going to be all over you. But the horse has to respect your space. You don't want them to be leaning toward you when you're modeling, or trying to get in your hand or your pocket. The horse can't think of you as their playmate all the time, and they have to respect that boundary.

You have to create a picture for the judge and you don't want to be in the picture, literally or figuratively. You don't want to be distracting with whatever little prop you have.

At Pony Finals, for example, kids can get nervous and start positioning and repositioning and moving. It's important to think of the timing of when to stand your animal up. You don't want to stand them up if the judge is ten ponies away. It's like riding in an under saddle class. You need to know where the judge is to help your horse peak at the right time. You're not going to walk in and immediately stand the horse up when there are twenty people in

> "When you're showing a model horse, they've got their space. The handler is not to be in their space. When you're trying to judge a model horse, you don't want to see the handler in the way." —CB

Riders at the far end of the ring model their ponies at Pony Finals.

the ring and one judge is at the front and the other one's at the back and you're in the middle. A horse or pony is only going to stand at attention for so long. You don't expect your horse to stand in the model for fifteen minutes, purposefully, the whole time. Think about having your animal stand in a model class for the ninety seconds or so that the judge is actually focused on them. Walk a circle and mix it up so your horse isn't bored.

You can tell who has prepared for the model and who hasn't even as they walk in the ring. In addition to walking with purpose, it comes down to the little things, like the way your bridle fits. How shiny is your bit? At Balmoral, we have separate model bridles with the bits sewn in. Bits and buckles are always shined the night before.

Most people, realistically, aren't going to do a model class, and there's nothing wrong with that. But learning the basics of good conformation if you're going to buy a horse—or just understanding your own horse's conformation—is part of being a good horseman.

CHAPTER 6
Tack and Equipment

OVER THE YEARS, we've developed a loyalty to several pieces of equipment and ways of approaching tack for our horses. Some of them have become our trademarks. But, like everything else we do, there is no one-size-fits-all approach. Each horse is an individual so we don't use any one piece of tack on every horse. It all comes down to what works for that particular animal.

Before we get into the specifics, we must note that every piece of tack that we use daily is cleaned daily. Bits are cleaned after every ride, but never in the dirty tack water where you dip your sponges (a pet peeve!). The care of your equipment is incredibly important because there is the safety factor to consider. If you're caring for your equipment on a daily basis, you'll be able to spot a problem in the making, primarily when it comes to stitching on your leather. If you can easily pull a stitch out from your leather, it may be rotten, and your tack is at risk of breaking while in use. A related guideline of ours, especially with your bridle, is that nothing is on the tightest, highest, last, or lowest hole. You want to have the ability to adjust. Sometimes leather stretches and you don't want to get to the ring and realize your bit is too low and not have the ability to adjust it.

OUR TACK TRADEMARKS
Saddles and pads

One of the things people tend to notice is our use of the big, white rectangular saddle pads. For many horses, depending on their shape, this type of pad can provide more cushion and make them more comfortable. The saddle sits where it needs to, and the pad does not bunch up. The pad forms to the horse because it's wider than your average English saddle pad. Every horse has different withers, and a different slope to their back. So the pad can fill in the voids where your saddle may not fit a horse perfectly. It's still an individ-

> "Over the years, we've often seen our riders together in the tack room, talking about their lessons or what was bothering them. But they never left the tack room unhappy. You could walk around the corner and hear them laughing. I think it's really important." —CB

ual consideration with the pads—for example, this type of pad may not work as well on ponies with a rounder shape. Always consider the individual animal.

For saddles, we worked with Butet® to design a Balmoral Butet and a Balmoral Pony saddle. We adjusted the center of balance further back, similar to an old-school close contact saddle—without feeling like a board! The panels are integrated and the base is wider. It puts your balance in a great spot, enabling you to sense and feel more of your horse. We've never used the knee and thigh blocks that have become so popular, even in the Butet saddles we used before designing our own. Blocks mostly just put you further away from the horse. The knee block in the front definitely puts more saddle between you and your horse, and you end up learning to brace against it. We believe that blocks don't give your leg the freedom to be where it wants to be, and essentially locks your leg in place. It's the whole bucket saddle mentality, with the deep seat and the blocks to hold you in. Unfortunately, that's really just a false sense of security. No saddle can hold you in, and we think you're a lot better off being able to wrap your legs down and around your horse. We want to become part of the horse, not to sit on top of it.

String girths

We are huge proponents of wider string girths. They expand and contract, eliminating the possibility of one pressure point on the horse's body. They distribute the pressure more evenly around the horse's sternum and rib area. Essentially, a string girth is likely to make a horse feel more physically comfortable. It's like if you have sore feet, and you can wear either high heels or athletic shoes with insoles. The latter is going to feel a lot better. The string girth, like comfortable human shoes, is not going to pinch or impinge. It allows the horses freedom in their shoulders, too.

Like any other piece of equipment, however, string girths are not one-size-fits-all. Some horses prefer a leather girth because they like the feeling of security that it provides. But when we use leather girths, we make sure that they are wide enough to cover more than one rib so that the girth does not slide or pinch. (We designed a wide leather girth to meet this need, too.) The human equivalent here would be a really thin, tight belt. You're not going to want to stand up super straight or run around and exercise if the belt is too tight or pinches you.

A word of warning about string girths: The whole idea of a string girth is that it gives. So, as you're riding, you need to check it more often than you would check another type of girth. As your horse gets warm or starts to sweat, you want to be sure your saddle isn't sliding. Also, be careful if you're wearing spurs while using a string girth, because it is possible to get a spur stuck (a work-around is to add a girth cover).

We can't repeat enough that each horse is an individual, so we advocate for making individual decisions about everything, including tack.

Nosebands

Soft rope nosebands are one of our trademarks now, like our white reins and white bit guards (also cleaned daily!). As we see it with nosebands, less is more. For schooling, many of our horses wear rope nosebands, or no noseband at all. If we do use a noseband, we always school with it loose.

You'll see some people who train with a drop noseband or a figure eight. We don't agree with the use of those nosebands in training because they inhibit the horse's ability to move their tongue, essentially tying the horse's mouth shut. This is treating a symptom, rather than addressing why the horse is opening their mouth. What is that horse going to do once the drop or figure eight noseband is removed? Open their mouth. But we want to teach horses to do the opposite. Plus, when a horse goes into the show ring in a different noseband, they're going to be a different ride. That's why we school with a noseband loose and, if we need to tighten it, we do so right before we enter the show ring. We don't ever want to force something on a horse, like forcing their mouth closed with tack. We want the horse to keep their mouth closed because they're happy, comfortable, and well-trained.

Bits

Horses need to be able to move their tongue on the bit. You want the horse to salivate because that's going to make them softer in your hands, softer on the bit, softer in their jaw, and more responsive and relaxed overall. And when horses are relaxed, they're more rideable and happier. Achieving this is yet another individual process.

Bit selection also comes down to this simple question: How does that bit feel in the horse's mouth? If you want your horse to take more hold, what should that feel like to the horse? If you want your horse to come back a little better or be a little softer in his jaw, what kind of bit would make the horse want to do that? Make sure your horse's teeth are done by someone you trust. And learn the basics of what's going on inside your horse's mouth. Take a flashlight and look inside. Is their palette low? Do they have a wider mouth? Are the bars narrow? Low? Wide? Sensitive? It's amazing how often we see bits pinching the corners of the mouth or sitting too low in the mouth. Each horse is unique, and if you pay attention, your horse will tell you what does and doesn't feel good in their mouth.

In choosing which bit to use for which horse, nothing is fixed. It's a completely individual choice, though the end goal is a common one: You want the horse to take a hold of you, to take contact with the bit, so that you can then have a conversation and communicate with the horse. We never want to over-bit, or to immediately go to stronger bits, if we are trying to make a change or solve an issue. Less is more. Start with less.

We find that a lot of mouth issues come from the horses not being responsive to the leg. It's often a forward issue. Think about when you pedal faster—your bike becomes easier to steer. As your horse goes forward, they become lighter. If your horse is leaning on your hand, is it because they're not strong behind? Or behind the leg? **A horse being strong and a horse being heavy are two different things.**

We like to mix it up and experiment with bits to keep things interesting. Maybe you've been riding your horse in a rubber snaffle and then you try a Happy Mouth Bit and you discover that your horse likes the new bit better. For us, it's about not getting into the, "My horse only goes in this bit" rut. You never know until you try, so we do a lot of experimenting (but never with harsh bits), just to keep the horse's mouth talking.

When you're working with a new bit for a horse, you'll want to make sure it is the proper width. And if it's any kind of jointed bit, make sure that it's not pinching the corners of the mouth. With a jointed bit, we will put a few wraps of latex tape on the joint to soften it up and encourage the horse to mouth it and salivate and suck on the bit a little. We change the latex tape frequently because, over time, it gets stale. Then, as a general rule, the horse won't want to suck on it as much. Replacing the latex weekly keeps it fresh. (Note: never put a bit with latex on it in the tack water!)

CLEANLINESS

We saved the best, or perhaps the most important, subject for last. It is so important that your tack is clean. The expectation for our riders before they come to the ring (at home or at the horse show) is that their turnout and their

Make tack cleaning one of your daily routines at the barn.

equipment are clean, clean, clean. And we believe that a clean presentation goes way beyond aesthetics.

If you, your horse, and your equipment are clean, it can actually boost your confidence. Cleanliness goes hand in hand with feeling organized, which plays right into feeling confident. You get almost a little head start when you feel prepared. Imagine that your tack is clean, your horse is clean, you've shined your boots, you've shined your stirrups, you've shined your bit ... it puts you one step ahead. When you prioritize cleanliness, you start off your ride feeling in control, which is important when so many other things are going to be outside of your control! *Control what you can in every area of horsemanship—like the details in your turnout—and it will help you to feel more prepared and confident.*

CHAPTER 7
Safety

YOU COULD WRITE an entire book on how to prioritize safety around horses. The fact is, life can be unpredictable. Horses can be unpredictable. You can't anticipate and plan for all possible situations, so the best thing you can do is to establish safe habits in every area of your horsemanship, and implement those habits every single time you're around or on a horse. Control what you can control—because there's plenty you can't! From how you lead your horse to how you stand at the mounting block, accidents happen from carelessness.

HELMETS

We'll start with the obvious—helmets. Believe it or not, safety helmets with harnesses have only been required for junior riders since 2001. Even later than that for adults. We've come a long way from the top hats and hunt caps of old, and safety measures are on the rise. (Please note: Photos of Carleton in this book without a proper headgear are merely a reflection of their time and not endorsed given current standards.)

Quite simply, it is our advice (and the advice of many horsemen) to wear a helmet every single time you're on a horse. And not just any helmet, but one that properly fits your head. Helmets should fit very snugly. People often want them to feel comfortable, but snug is key. It's not a baseball cap! Importantly, the brim should not interfere with your ability to lift your eyes. With a little time, most helmets will mold slightly to your head and feel like less of a squeeze. You don't want a helmet to be painfully tight, but loose and comfortable is a big no! If your helmet is a little loose, it will move if it hits the ground and it won't provide the protection intended.

Ideally, you want to get fitted by someone trained in helmet-fitting, in person, at a tack shop or a mobile tack shop at a horse show. We always defer to the professionals when it comes to fit. If that's not an option for you, follow the manufacturer's fit guidelines. One basic rule of thumb is when you move the helmet up and down on your head by the brim, your eyebrows should move up and down with it. If they do, you've likely got a decent fit.

Another note to keep in mind is that everyone's head is shaped differently. Certain helmets are designed to fit oval-shaped heads better, while other

> "Tradition changes, it evolves, and it has to evolve with increased knowledge and technology. The more people get used to seeing something, the more it gets integrated into what's normal for us. We didn't previously ride with harnesses on our helmets, but now that's standard. Everyone is getting used to vests and they have become an optional and acceptable part of the attire." —TB

helmets are designed for round heads. Just because a particular brand or style of helmet is on-trend or it looks good (there's a lot of this in the horse world!) doesn't mean it's going to be the safest helmet for you. Head shape is another reason to go to a professional whenever possible for a fitting. If your helmet hits the ground, stop wearing it immediately—you always want to replace your helmet after a fall. You can inquire with the brand about their replacement program—many brands will offer you a significant discount on a new helmet after a fall if you send the damaged one back to them.

As of the writing of this book, the Virginia Tech Helmet Lab had just begun independent testing of equestrian helmets—a huge milestone. The result of that testing is expected to be a five-star rating system, so consumers will have more knowledge about specific helmet brands and styles and how they performed in testing. (Currently, helmets only need to be ASTM-certified to be approved for competition.)

MIPS technology, which has been shown to reduce the risk of concussion, has also recently been incorporated in many helmet styles. Another welcome advancement in the evolution of riding helmets!

VESTS

At the time of this writing, safety vests (both the traditional body protectors and the newer airbag vests) have gained significant popularity in the show ring. For so long, you didn't see them in the ring ... but we also didn't wear our modern helmets in the show ring either! Safety is something that's always evolving with technology. And while it seems like tradition—historically prized in the horse show world—and safety are at odds with one another, they don't have to be. You can keep up tradition while making safety your top priority.

We believe that within the next few years, there will be a lot more research into air vests, and their popularity among riders will only continue to increase. We fully support this. Body protectors are a good option, too, for

> "If you want to wear a vest in the show ring, as a judge, I'm never going to fault you for it." —CB

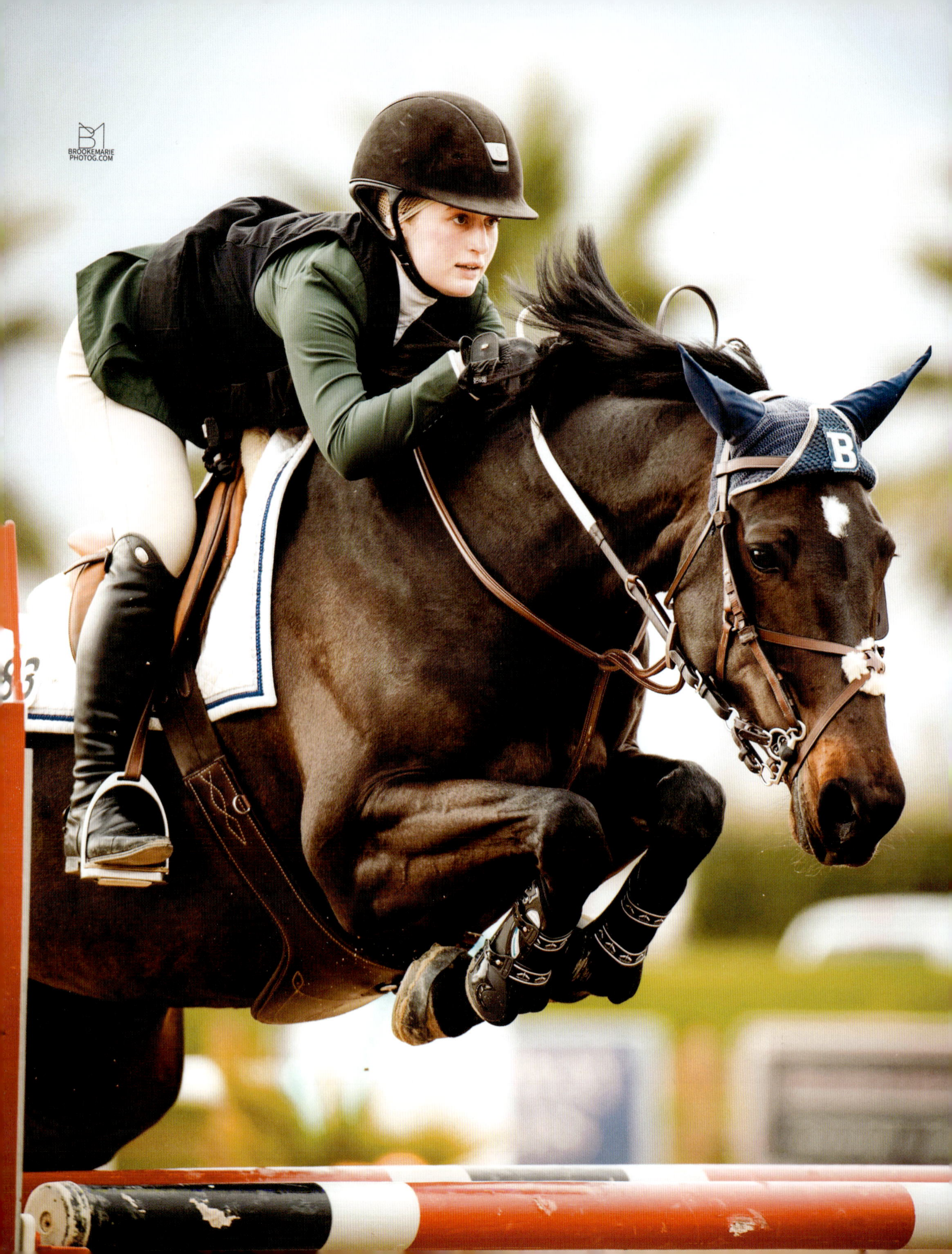
BROOKEMARIE
PHOTOG.COM
B
83

added protection in case of impact. Several options are very streamlined—you hardly notice someone's wearing one. The tradition is still there. The way we see it, if you wear your hunt coat with a body protector over it, you're still following tradition. It's just like wearing your hunt coat underneath a raincoat when it's pouring down rain. You're making a practical decision while still acknowledging tradition.

We are all for the safety of wearing body protection, and believe that if a body protector or an air vest makes you feel more comfortable, you should wear one. The added assurance and confidence this piece of equipment gives you could actually make your riding more effective. (Remember that the mental element of riding is huge.) Our stance is, if we have this new technology, we should use it.

It is worth mentioning, however, that you don't want a vest to give you a false sense of security. It's an additional safety measure, not a magic wand to prevent any accident or injury from ever happening. We once saw someone doing the jumpers while wearing a vest, and the parent of one of our junior riders was commenting on it. It seemed like this man was galloping at about six hundred miles an hour. This parent said, "Do you think having the vest gives him a false sense of security?" Again, a safety vest is only an additional precaution. The safest things you can do in your riding are to train with someone knowledgeable and listen to them on all topics: suitable horses for you, vet work, prep work, appropriate divisions for showing, and so on. There should be thought and reason—purpose—behind every decision.

MOUNTING, LEADING, AND TACKING

This is a big one for us when it comes to safety. Many people fall off or have accidents at the mounting block. The first rule of thumb is to be paying strict attention while mounting. It's so easy for a rider to be distracted, but what

Training your horse to stand at the mounting block—and being focused and efficient yourself—are key to staying safe.

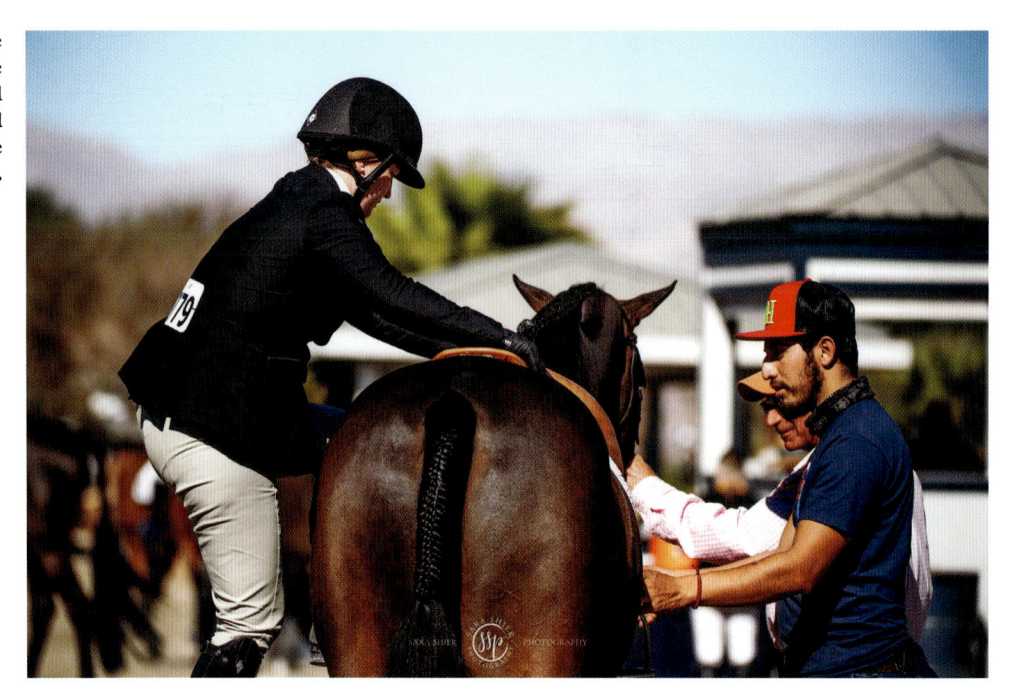

happens to a distracted rider and a horse that starts walking off prematurely? The rider tries to swing their leg over, but ends up nearly behind the saddle. Then the horse spooks and the rider is in no position to stop it.

Sometimes even professionals become absent-minded while mounting, or they don't insist that the horse stand for the whole mounting process. With too many horses, the moment you swing your leg over, off they go. Teach your horse to stand politely until you've settled into the saddle. If he doesn't, have someone hold him until he learns to do so.

Also keep in mind that the longer you stand at the mounting block, the more likely it is that something could happen. Someone comes up behind you, or makes a loud noise, or your horse gets antsy, or whatever the case may be. When you first get to the mounting block, your girth should be secure, your stirrups down, reins over the head, and you're ready to go as soon as your horse is in position. Don't tempt fate. Find your other stirrup as soon as you swing your leg over and sit down gently while mounting.

No detail is too small in any area of safety with horses.

For our newer riders, we start by teaching them the proper technique for leading the horse. If a horse is spooking, you should pull its head toward you, because then it can't spin around and kick you. We practice these basics over and over with our students so that, even before they get on the horse, they feel empowered, in control, and confident.

We emphasize to newer riders that you want to be acutely aware of where your body is in relation to the horse's body while you're tacking up. It's human nature to pick up bad habits, so even for more experienced horsemen, reminding and retraining yourself about safety habits on a regular basis can only help.

For example, when you bend down to wrap a leg, you want to be off to the side and not facing the horse's knee. Sitting on the ground or standing in front of the horse are mistakes that can result in people getting hurt. If a horse picks up his knee because he's got a fly on his leg, you're going to get that knee in the face—that's why we tell the riders who work with us that they always need to be scanning. This goes for the entire barn area, stalls, etc. Scanning, scanning, scanning the horses and your surroundings. So much of being safe around horses is just paying attention.

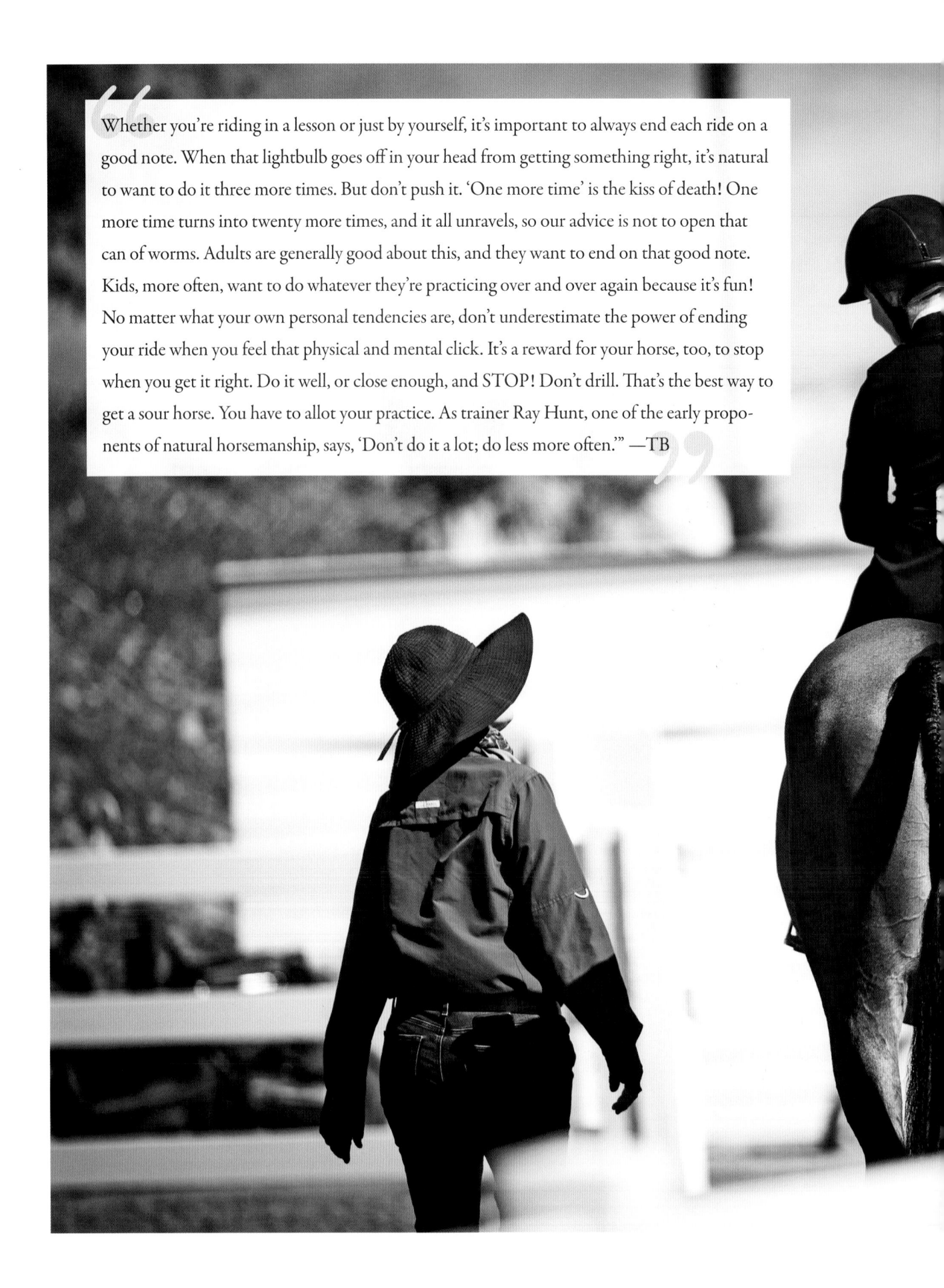

"Whether you're riding in a lesson or just by yourself, it's important to always end each ride on a good note. When that lightbulb goes off in your head from getting something right, it's natural to want to do it three more times. But don't push it. 'One more time' is the kiss of death! One more time turns into twenty more times, and it all unravels, so our advice is not to open that can of worms. Adults are generally good about this, and they want to end on that good note. Kids, more often, want to do whatever they're practicing over and over again because it's fun! No matter what your own personal tendencies are, don't underestimate the power of ending your ride when you feel that physical and mental click. It's a reward for your horse, too, to stop when you get it right. Do it well, or close enough, and STOP! Don't drill. That's the best way to get a sour horse. You have to allot your practice. As trainer Ray Hunt, one of the early proponents of natural horsemanship, says, 'Don't do it a lot; do less more often.'" —TB

PART II
On Training

"One thing I like to tell riders is that success literally comes from failure. When you're learning something new, you might have to fail at it over and over again before getting it right. Instead of looking at that through a lens of negativity, look at it as a positive. Truly, the more you make a mistake on your road to a new skill, the closer you are to being successful at that new skill. When you find yourself failing at something several times, try thinking to yourself, 'I'm that much closer to getting it!'" —CB

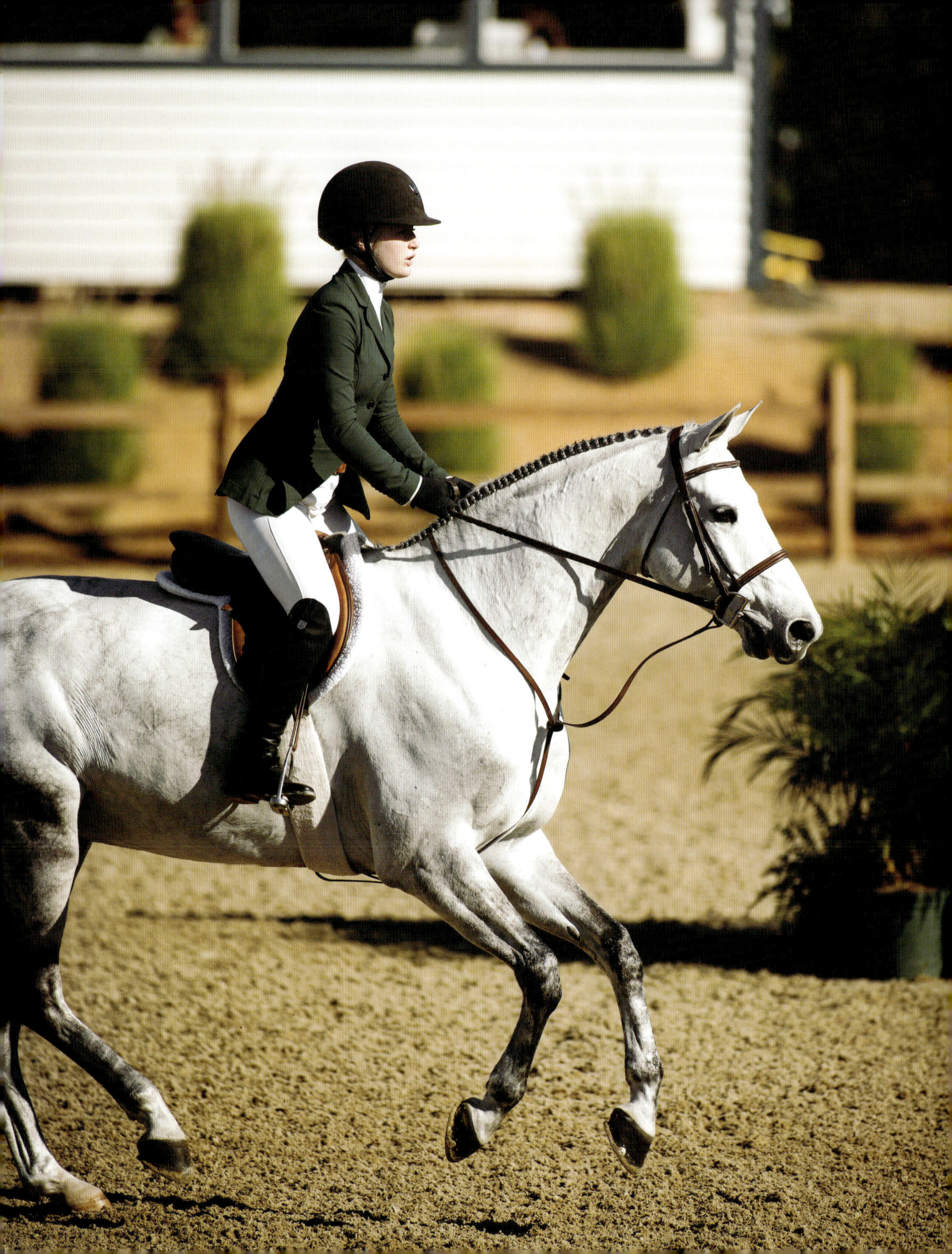

CHAPTER 8
The Importance of Forward

THE SINGLE MOST important thing you can do as a rider is to establish going forward on your horse. And you go forward as a team.

So, what does it mean to go forward?

A lot of people confuse going forward with speed. But going forward has nothing to do with an increase of speed or with going fast. When you increase your speed at a canter, or even at a walk, the stride might actually shorten. Going forward is about the horse's energetic step. The forward movement has to have purpose.

Forward is energy—that feeling of energy underneath you. A feeling of readiness and impulsion. Going forward is moving toward something ahead of you, moving toward a destination.

Visualize two-thirds to three-quarters of your horse out in front of you. Your horse should be carrying you. Taking you. They should feel light and energetic and ready, accepting the bit and the contact. A horse can't have impulsion and be truly forward without contact.

Think about the horse's engine, their power, coming from the back. Picture the hind legs as the pistons starting to fire. The hind legs get going, they come a little further underneath the horse's belly with each step, and that causes the belly and wither to come up, allowing the shoulders to swing more freely.

A forward pace is an irreplaceable foundation in the show ring.

More technically speaking, going forward means the hind end reaches up more before the front end lengthens. A lot of people want to lengthen the front end when they ask their horse to go forward. But then the horse actually gets more behind your leg and the balance lowers.

THE FOUR BASES OF SUPPORT

Before we start the how-to section of going forward, it's important to understand your four bases of support as a rider:

fig. 1 Your lower leg, from the knee joint, down
fig. 2 Your seat and thigh, from the hip down to the knee joint
fig. 3 Your upper body, which includes your arms and hands
fig. 4 Your head and eyes, for balancing and direction

fig. 1

fig. 2

fig. 3

fig. 4

With newer riders, we like to make it five bases of support because we separate the upper body as its own base, with arms and hands as another separate base. Initially, we don't want students to visualize their arms and hands being attached to their upper body. We always add the arms and hands into your riding last. It's human nature to want to pull on the reins first, but we actually want the opposite. Using your arms and hands should be the last thing you do. So mentally it helps novice riders to think of their arms and hands as a separate base from their upper bodies.

We like to teach visually this way so that you're thinking of your body on the horse, not as one unit, but as individual parts that each have their own job or function. It's like building blocks. Before you can execute something, you have to understand it, and that often means you have to be able to picture it.

Of all the bases of support, people generally consider their head and eyes the least—particularly their eye level on the horse. Most people, when they're thinking, they look down. But on a horse, that impacts the balance and actually puts more weight on the forehand. Think of having 65% of the weight on the hind end and 35% on the front.

Now let's return to that first base of support—your lower leg.

Think of your lower leg as the main method of communication with the horse. Always leg first. Your spurs, stick, and voice are all aids to your leg. Really digging in with both spurs at the same time is, in most instances, not what you want. Think about if someone stood behind you and squeezed or poked your ribs on both sides. Then, think about if someone gave you a push on alternating sides. Which feels better? What's your reaction to each? Don't insist on anything with your horse in a harsh way. Go together as a team. One leg at a time. Always think about how it feels to the horse.

The way we break that down for beginner riders is this: First, you have to learn to go forward and straight. Then we work on getting into the other gears.

> "A horse, when he thinks, actually lifts up. And if you are not mimicking your horse, you are not part of him as one unit. By looking down ourselves, we're contradicting what the horse wants to do. A lot of people want to get the horse's head down, but I encourage riders to give the horse a chance. When a horse is comfortable with their thoughts, they'll actually lower their head." —CB

> "I always say, if you're having a problem with straightness, pedal faster! Think about riding a bike and if you hit a patch of gravel and swerve. The way to get out of that trouble is to pedal faster. Same thing on a horse. Forward corrects many other issues. The answer is always to go forward. And forward = straight."—TB

We know that carrying some pace can feel scary, but to get comfortable with a correct, forward pace, you have to practice it. It's about positivity, promptness, readiness, and energy, not so much quickness or speed.

In every gait, there's nothing more important for a rider to think about than moving forward. Forward motion accomplishes most everything you might want to do in a ride, and can get you out of trouble as well.

Let's first discuss how we use the leg in order to get your horse in front of it. To begin, you're using your leg as a pulse to cue the horse. Then, if more pressure is needed, maybe a dull thump. When you apply pressure, your horse should yield to that pressure. And you only want to apply as much pressure as is needed at any given moment. If the horse responds to the pulse, there's no need to thump.

What about the use of a cluck or a stick? If you don't get the desired response, you want to follow this order: leg, cluck, stick. You want to train the

> "If someone took a photo of you, it should look like there is literally more horse in front of your leg than behind it. You can visualize three-quarters of the horse in front of your leg and one-quarter behind it. Ride into the picture you're creating for yourself and keep going forward." —CB

> "In all your riding, think about encouraging the horse forward and having them reach for the bridle. I like to use less bridle whenever possible. As I ask a horse to come up, I continue to raise my hands up to maintain that soft, flexible contact." –CB

horse to the cluck so they know that if they don't respond to the leg, they get a cluck. If they don't respond to the cluck, they get a little stick so they associate the leg with reacting to move forward. It's clearly understood, and it's a pattern. The stick is not always a punishment. Sometimes you'll see us walk a horse and just lightly tap with each step, like a metronome to keep a rhythm.

Again, you don't want to dig in with both spurs at the same time because the horse will resist. The spur is an aid to your leg, not so much a tool in and of itself. It's a pet peeve of ours when riders jab both spurs in, sliding their leg back and raising their heels to use the spur. So, with your whole lower leg, you cue the horse to travel at the desired pace, then over the pace, before settling in to where we ultimately want to be. That tells the horse, "We're confident and we're gonna do this!" Sometimes we use the term "shove 'em up," since it helps a rider visualize moving the horse in front of their leg. This tells your horse, "Oh, she really means it, let's go!"

Horses are flight animals. It is their natural instinct to evade pressure. This is why it's so important to set yourself down and around the horse, settling yourself into the saddle and melting into the movement. Picture the horse's hind legs coming under and the belly coming up.

GOING FORWARD AT THE WALK

First thing's first: the walk. We find the walk to be the most important gait, and an underutilized one for training your horse. The walk is the perfect time to get your horse in gear and in tune with you for what's ahead.

Start by lengthening and shortening your horse's stride at the walk only. Try using one leg three times—thump, thump, thump, and tapping with the stick if the horse doesn't listen—and then the other leg: thump, thump, thump. Or, you can alternate left leg, right leg, left leg, and so on. The goal is to get your horse forward and attentive at the walk. Before long, all you need to do is insinuate that you're going to close your leg, and the horse should step right up to you.

GOING FORWARD AT THE TROT

At home, at the start of a lesson or training ride, we might not do much trotting initially, particularly with a lazier horse. After lots of prompt walking, we like to have riders get up into a half seat and jog a few laps, possibly trot some large figure eights, then canter or even hand-gallop a couple of laps. Only then do they go back to trotting, so they're not constantly nagging the horse at the trot. After you canter or gallop, your horse will stretch and wake up. They'll be more attentive and in front of you, and you'll have something to work with when you drop back to trotting. Think of the downward transition as a forward movement. Also, we want to get the horse's heart rate up, which we can achieve by going through their entire range of motion.

When you are working at the trot, think about posting closer to the horse as a way to push your horse out further in front of you. Imagine that you're physically shoving the saddle out in front to open up your horse's front end on the upbeat, rather than standing up and sitting down in the saddle. And then on the down beat, add leg. Picture the hind legs coming farther up under the belly with each step while the shoulders reach farther ahead. During this, the horse is moving into your hand, reaching for the bit.

GOING FORWARD AT THE CANTER

Horses understand things in a progression. So rather than simply telling a horse to "GO!" when it's time to canter, we refer to our motto: suggest, rehearse, execute. You don't want to surprise your horse. This motto applies to everything you ask of your horse while riding, but let's apply it to the canter first. It's almost another way of saying "ready, set, go!" If you're heading toward a stop sign in your car, you don't just step on the brake when you get there. You have the picture painted in your mind's eye of what you're going to do before you slow down the car; it's the same with a horse—you paint the picture before you ask them to do something.

Think about reaction time. Say your horse weighs 1200 lbs. How quickly can a thought go from your brain, to your body, to the horse's body, to the horse's brain? It's certainly not instantaneous. So, when you're ready to move your horse up, you're going to suggest, rehearse, then execute. If someone asks you to do something, you pause. On a horse, if you suggest and then rehearse first, when it's time to

> "In mental and physical conversation with a horse, I never stop thinking and talking, without actually speaking." —CB

execute, he'll most likely go when you ask. Just like you'd be more amenable to doing something if it's suggested and rehearsed first.

Think about the horse receiving what you're asking when it's time to step into the canter:
Suggest the canter: *Nah, I don't want to.*
Rehearse asking for the canter: *Ehhhh, well, maybe.*
Execute the canter transition: *Okay, I'll do it.*

The horse needs to understand what you're asking for in order to crisply step up into the new gait. Ask yourself, "If I asked my horse to canter right now, would he jump right into it?" If the answer is no, you're not ready. Suggest and rehearse asking for the upward transition. Afterward, if you feel the horse would step right up into the canter, then you're ready to execute. Preparation is key.

We like to correlate it to a dance. Everything is flow and rhythm. Just like driving a car or walking your dog. If you simply ask your horse to turn left, you may feel a little resistance, and then they follow your lead. We try to eliminate that hesitation—that moment of pause—by doing things in steps: Suggest it, rehearse it, then execute it. It's an artistic endeavor we're trying to achieve.

In other words, have your plan before the moment it needs to happen. Think about it as three or four horse lengths ahead. Tell yourself, "That's when I'm going to start to ask," whether you're asking for a transition to the

> "It's a pleasant conversation with your horse. There's always a back and forth." —CB

canter, a turn, or whatever. Set it up, suggest it in advance, then do it. You'll feel your horse respond much better than if you just ask for something out of nowhere. Picture cantering down the rail, and suddenly you say, "TURN NOW!" That's going to surprise your horse and you're not going to get anything smooth or soft from them. The suggest, rehearse, execute method is about having a constant conversation with your horse as a member of their herd. You should always be thinking about what's next, and where you're going next, so you can ask your horse with the proper preparation. (Remember: We do everything with purpose!)

In the canter, you can also think about the idea that your stride has a front and a back. When you're creating that forward energy, picture your stride like a box. Your horse's front legs are in the front of the box, and the back legs in the back of the box. As you're thinking "rhythm" (speed + stride length + energy = rhythm) and "straight," you can also visualize that box and try to replicate it so that every stride is the same length. You want to think to yourself, "This is what a 12-foot stride feels like," and picture the size of that box, keeping your stride inside it. If you want to be on a 10-foot stride, picture how the box compresses to be 10 feet long and what your horse's stride feels like compressed into that space. The horse's head will come up, the hind end comes under, and the stride gets bouncy.

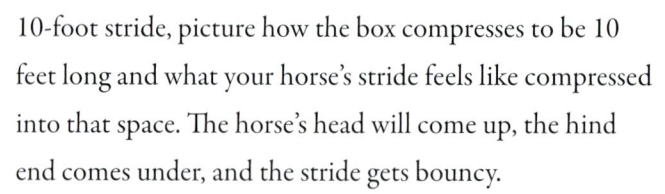

GOING FORWARD TO THE FIRST JUMP

In your over fences classes, you have to get to that first jump with positivity. Tell your horse a couple of times on your approach to that first jump that you're determined to be positive. Otherwise the horse may not be attentive. They don't know the course or what you're thinking, or even that there is a first jump!

> "Instead of 'sitting,' think about 'setting' yourself on your horse. Posting is nothing more than setting yourself back into the saddle in the same place every stride. You're never sitting heavily without meaning to, never sitting without being in control of how much you're sitting, and never sitting on the back of your seat, where your jeans pockets would be, unless you're consciously driving the horse forward. You can change your seat stride to stride. This takes a lot of thigh and core strength and proper leg position, and it's about having consistent and constant body control." —TB

Get over/above the pace in the warmup ring. To visualize getting over the pace, think about bringing your horse up to, say, 15 mph, then ease them down to 10, and then maintain your canter at 12 mph. (Please note: we are not suggesting you literally travel at the above speeds! They are just meant for visualization purposes and other numbers can be used as well—whatever helps you picture and feel the differences in pace. You can also use a scale of 1-5, or 1-10, or whatever helps you to "work the gears.") Go through the process of setting your pace in the warm up, and again as you set your pace to the first jump in the ring.

HOW TO SET YOURSELF IN THE SADDLE

You want a generous response from the horse when you ask to move forward—maybe even "extra" as you're getting started and working on your horse's responsiveness. To achieve that, you want to set yourself around your horse, rather than to sit atop him. If you've got a slow or reluctant horse underneath you when you pick up the canter, post up a couple of times (not to be confused with "posting the canter," which we don't encourage as a regular practice), and

> "Great riders take the time to sit straight." —CB

> "I use different seats at the canter throughout a course of jumps. I never use a truly deep seat because I never try to dominate the horse. If I'm setting down into the saddle, I'm always allowing my body to move with the horse in a following motion." —CB

shove the horse up in front of you. Your knee needs to bend 55-60 degrees when setting in the saddle.

Think about the connection of your seat, seat bones, and your weight more than sitting. The connection is fluid so that you can rock into one hip and thigh depending on what you're trying to accomplish. It's always more thigh and hip than seat when you're in the saddle.

You can also ask yourself, "Where would I be if I dropped the reins while asking the horse to go forward?" Your core would engage, your hip angle would close, and your head and eyes would come up. It happens automatically. Your light seat implies "go" to the horse. When you really sit hard, the horse can't bring their front end up. They become inverted, with their belly low. Slide your seat bones back to set yourself in the saddle and bend your knees more. Going forward means sliding your seat bones back and adding more connection, closing your thigh. You can lighten your seat bones without losing their contact with the saddle. Get comfortable with going forward and, whenever you need to, remember that the answer is often just to "pedal faster!" Be with your horse as they respond. Make sure you're ready by not falling behind the motion as your horse moves forward.

It also helps to think about staying centered on your horse: half your body on one side, half on the other. Let your body drop down and you will stay centered, like ice cream melting around the horse evenly on both sides. It seems obvious for us to say you should stay centered on the horse, but it's actually really easy for riders to favor one side or the other, or to be stronger in one leg than the other. Sitting straight and centered, left to right and front to back, should be part of that (very long!) mental checklist in the saddle.

YOUR HANDS

Remember how one of the four bases of support is your upper body? Or, for riders with less experience, how your hands are the fifth base of support? We will discuss the riders' hands for the remainder of this chapter, as the incorrect use of your hands is not only a common problem, but also a real roadblock to going forward.

If someone's nervous, they typically start shortening or pulling on the reins, but the irony is, you're literally hanging on by a thread when you do that. The reins are not what's holding you anywhere, but that's human nature—the need for control and a feeling of security. It takes repetition and confidence to not grab for the reins. It's a safety default for humans on a horse to take the reins and stop—it's a feeling of control, or "I could stop if I needed to." But the answer, as you know, is actually to go forward. (Do we sound like a broken record yet?)

At Balmoral, we generally refer to five separate rein aids: direct, indirect, opening (i.e. guiding), neck rein (Western style, in which the rider moves both hands in or both hands out), and pulley rein. There are also times when you're riding that you can use a driving rein. This is not an aid per se but can be a helpful training tool.

DIRECT REIN Used when you're learning how to ride. A direct rein will bend the neck and change the direction of the horse, but it's also going to slow the horse down.

INDIRECT REIN If you're trying to move the horse over or get them to shape out or in, you'd use the indirect rein. Use this when you're trying to move the horse's whole body. The indirect rein will move the horse's body more laterally.

OPENING REIN This will help lead the horse and insinuate the direction that you want to go, without taking away any forward momentum.
NECK REIN Use a neck rein in addition to a direct rein to reinforce certain aids, particularly while turning or setting the horse back on their haunches.
PULLEY REIN Used in case of emergency; if a horse is running away with the rider.

To use a driving rein, you turn your hands over, like you're driving a carriage. The reins just lay across the top of your hand. We use this for a lot of reasons, like if the rider pulls, or the horse pulls, or if we're teaching a rider to understand how to use their arm and elbow correctly. We also like to break it down this way: When you pull, the pulling is not from your hand, but from raising your shoulders and bending your elbow. We talk a lot about the elbow because that's where connection begins.

Another unorthodox method we use (under careful supervision!) to help a rider stop pulling is taking the reins like you're going to lead the horse from the ground—under the neck—and hand them to the rider that way (using a driving rein). You just can't drop them! When you use the reins upside down like this, you mechanically cannot pull on the horse's mouth. It can be an illuminating exercise to learn about your tendencies with your hands and arms. Even if you just do it at the walk.

You can bridge your reins, too, when you need a refresher about riding with both reins. There's an effective bicycle handlebar analogy here—if you're riding your bike and you pull on the left handlebar only, what's going to happen if you don't have a hold of the other? Bridging the reins can help you to better feel and visualize that concept.

We like to tell riders that you're always using two reins. Sometimes one more than the other, but never one or the other. When you're thinking about using both of your hands, keep the following in mind:

- Take the rein away from the horse's neck when you're using the hand on that side—there's rarely a reason to push your hand into the neck.
- Think about forming a triangle from the horse's nose to each of your hands while you're holding the reins. In general, your hands should be the width of the bit so you can ride and feel both sides. Imagine the horse's nose as one point of the triangle, and your hands as the other two points. This might come up with a rider who has a tendency to hold her hands too close together. As you're thinking about the horse's nose as that point of the triangle between your hands, you're using your eyes and legs as guidance to send the horse's whole body into straightness from tail to nose. We find that riders can be so focused on the horse's head that they forget about the rest of the animal's body. If you hold your hands too close together, making the triangle too narrow, your horse's shoulders will move outside the line of your reins.
- If you think of the rein as a boundary or a guideline, you don't want your horse's shoulder to go outside of it, unless you have a specific reason for doing so. If your horse is bulging or drifting, the first correction would be to make sure the horse's

> "It's a lift-and-ease-off motion. When I go to pull up, reduce the speed, or to collect, I lift my shoulder, my arms bend more, my hands follow, and then I ease off the pressure through my arm and relax my shoulders. Then the horse actually responds and comes back." —CB

shoulder, rib cage, and hip stay in alignment—slightly to the inside of the boundary your reins have created.
- Keep equal space between the rein and the horse's neck on each side unless there's a reason to do otherwise.
- Use your eyes and legs to keep your horse in the center.
- Picture sending the tail right up through the middle of the chute you just created, all the way to the horse's nose.

We use a lot of analogies when teaching. As a trainer, if you explain why the rider is more likely to remember. And if they can picture it, they can understand it. It has to make sense.

If you exaggerate carrying your hands up off the neck, about where your belt buckle is, or a little higher as you ride your horse around (especially when you're walking), the horse will tend to bring their sternum up and start to carry their balance up. This makes them more free in their hind legs as they dig in and push. When riders put their hands down into the wither, the horses actually push away from that. They'll follow your hand. If you lift your hand, they'll lift their sternum up, their balance comes up,

> "As you're riding around and your shadow is in front of you with the sun on your back, you should not be able to see light between the sides of your body and your elbow." —CB

and they lighten and move forward more easily.

Also, before starting to actually draw on their mouth, you should slightly lift, re-lift, and lift again. As you lift, the horse will actually take contact into your arm and rein and accept it as if it's their idea, not yours. A lot of horses lean on the bridle because they're not strong behind, whether that's due to a deficiency in fitness, balance, natural ability, breeding, rider error, or a combination of those factors. Or, the rider may carry their hands too low (sometimes trying to be "smooth" or "subtle" or "stay out of the way," which can become detrimental to the horse being light, forward, and balanced).

When you need to slow your horse down, before you even add your hands into the equation, try slowly letting out a big breath and settling in. Even if this doesn't slow your horse down on the spot, it can prepare them for what's coming. You're making the suggestion of slowing down with your body before your hands ever get involved. Anytime you think about using the reins, your leg should be active and you should feel sturdy and anchored. Use the reins from contact, just by bending your elbow. If your reins are droopy or slack, your pull becomes a jerk.

For one of our riders who was working on her hands, we knotted the end of her reins so she could ride without them. As she was cantering around, she started playing with how to turn her body and guide her horse without pulling. You have to add your hands last. Everything can happen without your hands, and even if you need your hands the tiniest bit, that's going to be the final step. First, you're going to do other things. You're going to raise your eyes and set in. You're going to take a breath. Then maybe, if you need to, bend your arm a little more. But everybody likes to go to the reins first. People seem to visualize it pretty well if you say, "What would your position be if you just dropped your reins?" Think about that with jumping, too, and where you'd be in front of the jump, over the jump, and landing from the jump. If you're secure enough to jump with your reins knotted (again—under careful supervision!) try that next.

The more people feel like they are secure and confident on a horse, the more likely they are to be able to maintain light, soft hands. At Balmoral, we do a lot of jumping with one hand to work toward that security. We had one rider who had a tendency to be a little rough with her hands. She was a nice rider and on a really trusty horse, so we tried tying her reins in a knot for a bit of each ride. Again, the question you always want to be asking yourself is, "Where would I be if I had no hands? Where would I be if I took my hands off the reins? What would my position do if my horse sped up, if my horse slowed down? Where would I be?" Good hands come from having a strong base of support through your legs and core, and eliminating your hands from the equation helps you to truly focus on those other bases of support.

Safety note: Any time you plan on riding without reins, you must tie your reins in a knot. *Never* just drop them on the neck or you risk the reins going over your horse's head and potentially tripping them.

CHAPTER 9
Notes on Flatwork

EVERYONE LOVES JUMPING, but the vast majority of what we do is flatwork. If you think about being on course for two minutes, how much of that time is actually spent jumping? Ten or twelve seconds? The rest of it is nothing but flatwork, with hurdles in the way. Good jumps come from good flatwork and a responsive horse. So, if there's anywhere to focus your efforts in the saddle, it's on your flatwork. For most people, it should be a good three-quarters of the work you do at home, if not more. But without drilling. It's a fine line to keep it interesting for the horse and rider.

Riding in general comes down to four basics—calm, straight, forward, and square—in everything you do. To get a little bit more specific about your flatwork, you want to think about your horse maintaining rhythm, relaxation, connection, and with impulsion coming from back to front. Connection doesn't always mean contact; it can simply mean the relationship between you and your horse.

As an homage to Carleton's note-taking (We are talking about hundreds of notebooks!), we've organized this chapter and the next, "Notes on Jumping," as literal, individual notes. The following are some of our favorite pieces of advice, in note form, for getting the most out of your flatwork.

CB with his trusty notebook.

"One of the analogies that our riders have come to love is the idea of the horse being Jello in a pan. How do you get the Jello to move only to the left when you shake the pan? What are you doing with your body to influence the Jello? You always want the Jello to be flimsy, supple, and elastic in order to influence the way it moves with your body." —CB

BENDING AND TURNING

- The idea of bending can easily be misconstrued. So for us, it begins (like everything!) with straightness. Straightness is balance. Straightness is power. If you see a horse loose in a field, they're not bent when they go around a corner—they actually have their head turned to the outside for balance. When you bend a horse, you want its whole body to be on the track you're riding, from the back of the horse to the front. That's what we mean by straightness. It's a very common mistake to bend from front to back. Bending your horse's head and neck is incorrect. The bend is at the ribcage, not the neck. When you're thinking about the horse's whole body bending, imagine riding your bike through a turn. You turn the handlebars to go through a corner, but then you straighten back out. You don't keep the front wheel tilted to the inside.

- When thinking about a bend, imagine that the horse's outside nostril is over the point of the outside shoulder, even through a turn. That way, the horse doesn't lean in. That's a helpful visual, even if it isn't literally the way a horse's body is lined up. What you're aiming for is a firmer base for the horse on the outside feet so the inside feet can be lighter and actually turn first. And that has to start from behind. The outside rein is very important in achieving this.

- The train track analogy is also helpful for a lot of riders. If you're bending your horse in, you're getting a little bit on your inside wheels. And you're actually shortening your stride and putting your horse off balance to the

> "It's always two reins. A lot of times, it's one more than the other, but it's always two. You don't want to pull your horse off its train track. When you're coming out of a turn, you want the horse's balance to be over all four legs, equally." —CB

inside. Bending or pulling your horse in creates minimal weight on its outside legs and too much on the inside. We actually try to avoid the term "bending" through a turn, especially for more beginner riders. Try to think of it more like this: As you're going around a turn, your horse is straight, but they're shaped in the direction that they're going and looking in that direction. Of course, we want our horses to be supple and move off our leg and follow our hand. But we don't get fixated on the bend. Think of a turn as starting from the outside—guiding the horse's outside ribs and shoulder to the train track you want to end up on, and elevating the inside.

- Other trainers might explain this in another way, so you may hear this concept with different language from your trainer. This is our system and our terminology—it's not the only system or terminology. At the end of the day, it's all about the balance across the four legs, and the horse's outside legs providing an anchor for the inside legs. The outside is the anchor for the inside.
- People want to bend their horses from the shoulder forward, but the bend should actually come from the horse's hip and then through the rib cage. Work on the flexibility through the horse's body underneath your legs, not in front of them. When you ask for a bend, your outside leg and rein show the horse how far to go. Otherwise, the inside bend can result in the outside bulge.

> "When you ride a horse, think of it from the nailheads of the horse's shoe upwards, and not from where you're sitting, from the top downwards." —CB

YOUR BODY AND POSITION

- As you ride, if you slow your motion and slow your breathing down, the horse slows down. If you want to slow your horse down at the trot, think about posting more slowly and deliberately, rather than just keeping up with your horse's pace. You set the pace. A fun exercise is to post up, down, down, and notice whether your horse slows down.
- Always try to rebalance your seat bones so you're setting yourself equally in the saddle with the right and left sides of your seat. Most riders like to ride with one leg farther forward and straighter. Add that to your (very long and constantly scrolling!) mental checklist.
- Look straight between the horse's ears. Never drop your eye off to the side. Your chin should always be level with the top of their head, not lower to the horse—basically parallel to the ground. If needed, you can exaggerate this a bit. It's not just eyes up, it's chin up.
- A better way to describe heel position is saying your heel should be lower than the stirrup. Not that your heel is lower than your toe, because your heel could still be equal with the stirrup and that's not ideal. There needs to be pressure on the stirrup as well, since this is what anchors you. Think: "My heel is lower than the stirrup."

LAZY VS HOT HORSES

- One of the hardest types of rides is the slow horse. You're constantly working to keep that type of horse going. So, on days that you're only riding on the flat, make sure your horse is extra responsive to your leg. Sometimes if you amp up your own excitement and your own heart rate, it can amp the horse up, too. Once your horse is nice and warmed up from walking, try this: Step right into the canter and hand-gallop the long sides of the ring. Go for an overreaction to amp them up, then go back to trotting. Sometimes a horse can be sulky because they're bored, not sour. A change of scenery works wonders, too. Even just a walk around the property can freshen them up. Or sometimes it can help to hop a jump to get their attention and their energy up, and then go back to flatting.
- For lazy horses—or really, any horse—do lots of transitions from the walk to the trot and canter and back down again. You want them responsive to your leg immediately. Canter on a straightaway and then halt. Then walk and turn on haunches. Let the horse stretch at their own pace in a canter or gallop. Ask for even more pace than you'd want before going down to the trot.
- It's about getting this type of horse to be a little extra responsive so that they're light and active. You want to get a little extra pace, and then you can back off and be more subtle because you're getting the response. You can gallop a little bit to get your horse above the pace, then settle back into a medium pace. We like to do that a few times in a row, forward and back, forward and back, so that we know we have those gears and our horse is responsive. You want to feel like if you touched your horse with your outside leg, they'd step right into the canter. That's the feeling you're going for—that the horse is on alert, waiting for their cue, always ready.
- For the hotter type of horse, or the more sensitive type, we try not to wind them up. You don't want to get their heart rate too elevated. We want to unwind them. If that means spending an entire flat session just walking—moving laterally off the leg, and extending and condensing the stride at the walk—so be it. Build in times to let them pause and take a breath. Work that into your program.

- You also want to watch the level of adrenaline that you're building over the course of a ride. Build in walking breaks so the horse can take a breath. Let them stand and just watch what's going on in the ring. You're always wanting to create opportunities for them to settle and relax.
- Just the act of sinking down into the tack and letting a big breath out yourself can help your horse deflate. Almost as if you were planning on letting out the reins to walk on a loose rein. It's about teaching horses how to pause.

MIX IT UP

- On the days that you're flatting, you want to be sure to include plenty of variety. Every ride on the flat shouldn't be the same. We are huge advocates of getting out of the ring. If you can, find some hills to go up and down. Or even just walk along a trail. Don't do the same warmup every day—some days get right into your canter. The more you can mix it up, the better. Nothing is set in stone, and nobody says that you have to trot before you canter or that you have to go both directions. Try different things. Instead of trotting or cantering repetitive laps around the ring, use the quarter line and the center line, circle around jumps, and do simple changes on a straight line. Do a pretend course without jumps and just canter next to them, keeping track of your strides. Ride bareback to shake things up, or even with just a halter and lead rope if you have a horse and a setup where you can do that safely. We have treadmills at all of our barns to try to provide variety for our horses as well. If you did the exact same workout every day, wouldn't you get bored?

DOWN-SHIFTING

- When you're in the show ring, you're going to want to finesse your down-shifting—those times when your horse has picked up the pace and you want to ease them back down to a medium canter. Try practicing this at home so that you have it at your disposal in the show ring: Open your outside rein more and more as to not be obvious about your downshifting. It's a better and more subtle way to balance than using direct pressure on the bit. Remember that your outside rein is your balancing rein. By taking the horse's nose to their outside shoulder for a step or two, your horse will settle and pause. Take a breath while you do it.

LEAD CHANGES

- A lead change is hind end first. Riders can get so worried about the change that they sometimes forget about the hind end. So it's helpful to break it back down to those basics, those building blocks. Think about cantering toward the corner, changing leads on a straight line, and then turning. Changing leads and turning are generally not happening at the same time because as soon as you start to turn your horse's front end in, the hind end goes out (or stalls), and that outside hind leg can't push to change leads. You want to visualize the outside hind leg moving between the two front legs, not to the outside of them. Then you'll want to continue straight for two or three strides after the change.

- If you have a horse that's worried about lead changes, has a difficult change, or is just learning flying lead changes, you don't want them to get frazzled or worry about the change, either. Make it the horse's idea. When practicing, sometimes we'll canter across the diagonal and as we approach the corner, we'll start to collect, get the canter bouncy and animated, push the haunch in, and then halt or trot. Then we give the horse a pat and pick up the new, correct lead, or even just walk at that point. This way, the horse learns to bring their hind end under them to begin the process of changing.

- We don't practice lead changes too much on the flat, specifically not in the center of the ring. And particularly not for horses that have a good lead change already. We do downward transitions shifting their haunch to the inside. With horses like that, we prefer to leave them alone and save the changes for when we need them. When you practice lead changes too much and your horse gets almost too good at them, they can start to anticipate the change. Then you may get extra lead changes where you don't want them.

- If you were to get into the habit of exercising your horse and doing lead changes across the diagonal in the center of the ring, what's going to happen when you canter across the diagonal in the show ring on your way to the single oxer? Your horse is going to do what you've been training them to do and change leads on the way there. When we do want a lead change across the diagonal, we wait until we're closer to the turn and then ask the horse. We make sure the horse waits until they're asked so they don't start to anticipate the change. Sometimes we hold the lead and then pull up to the trot or walk so the horse is tuned in to what we're asking, rather than anticipating.

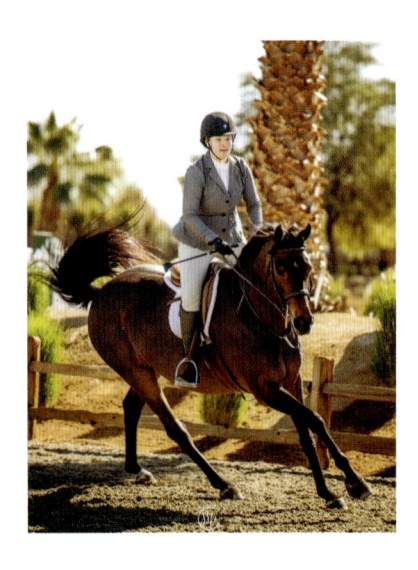

A FINAL NOTE ON CANTER PACE

- One way to get a feel for your canter paces (collected, medium, and extended) is to canter through two rails set on a line and see how many strides you do. If you get seven strides, the next time you do six. And the next time you do eight. Then go back and do seven again. That way you learn to set your pace in the corner, how to figure out the right canter to do the add, to leave out a stride, or to do the medium pace. When you do this with poles or cavaletti it's so much easier, mentally, because they aren't "real" jumps.

  DISCLAIMER: We do exercises with rails on the ground primarily for our more beginner riders. If you're at a more intermediate or advanced level, we recommend doing these types of exercises with small jumps or cavaletti because riding to a pole gets your focus low, which can then impact your horse's balance.

- As we wrap up this chapter and move into notes on jumping next, it's important to remember that a jump is just an elevated canter stride. Riders tend to make the jump an event when it's really just another stride. You wouldn't just be cantering down the long side of the ring and either speed up or start pulling for no reason. So why do that on the approach to a jump?

CHAPTER 10
Notes on Jumping

HORSES ONLY HAVE so many jumps in them. And so many shows. So one of our guiding principles when it comes to jumping is to budget your jumps wisely. This will help to keep your horse happy, comfortable, and willing. At Balmoral, we don't jump that often or that high when we're schooling at home.

When training over fences, you always want your horse to take you to the jump. Not the other way around. No matter the size of the jump, your horse must take you there.

That said, provided your horse has the athletic ability to jump, the size of the fences does not matter too much. People tend to get caught up in the height that they're jumping. Other than teaching your horse to gauge the height of the jumps, or to get the horse's muscles elastic to a certain height, it's simply not about the size of the obstacle. If you check all the boxes, it's the same formula, no matter how big the jumps might be. Rhythm, track, and pace are your cornerstones for jumping. When you've got the appropriate canter rhythm and pace while riding your horse straight on the chosen track, the jumps will come up for you. It's as simple as that. (We know, we know, it doesn't feel that simple! But hopefully these notes will be useful.)

WHAT ARE YOU JUMPING?

- We jump a variety of different types of jumps at home—a lot of solid walls and barrels. You always want to encourage your horse to jump up and around the jumps, to really pull their shoulders and belly up, and find their arc across the jump. We find that if we give them a more substantial jump, they are more likely to do this. The more substantial jumps may look imposing to the rider… but to a horse, they're actually more inviting. Most horses will want to take you to them more because they can see it and judge it better.

- Our horses jump barrels laid on their side at home specifically because the shape and the solid look helps them learn to jump around the jump and finish their arc. We suggest the use of barrels for schooling at home to encourage a round jump.

- Make sure you have ample ground lines because you want to give your horse room to get their legs up and to make that arc over the jump. It will also give some horses more confidence when they've got a solid ground line. Even with jumpers at home, we will use ground lines, whether it's a flower box or a rail on the ground. You don't want to trap your horse to train them.

- We don't use many wing standards at home. At a horse show, wing standards can funnel horses in and also encourage a better jump. We like to think that the wing standards give the horse more to look at, which is what encourages them to study the jump more, producing that added brilliance in the show ring. At home, wing standards also take up a lot of space in a smaller ring. You can fit more jumps without wing standards, plus it's easier to move and adjust the jumps with just upright standards.

- We also jump many of our lines at home from oxer to vertical, not vertical to oxer. We want to encourage our horses to jump around the first part of the line, so we practice at home jumping the oxer first, so that translates to a quality jump over the vertical at the horse show. You'll see a lot of horses jump oxers well, but they might not jump verticals quite as well. We want them to jump the vertical in the show ring a little more like it's an oxer—to rock back and jump slowly, explosively, up and around.

- We don't use a lot of fill and flowers at home. Our jumps aren't fancy or very colorful. That way, when we get to the show ring, the jumps are interesting to the horses and they study them and produce a more brilliant jump. One of the exceptions is that if we have a horse that's come from Europe, that horse may need to learn to jump flowers at home before we go to a horse show. This goes back to the individual considerations for every horse. You also wouldn't want to jump only rails at home and then have your horse feel over-faced by all the fill at a horse show. You want your horse to take you to the jump, study it, and jump with some brilliance, which they'll do because they're used to jumping interesting, more solid jumps at home (even if the home jumps are on the plain side). Studying a jump means respecting and measuring it—not sucking back from it or spooking. It's a fine line.

"When you've got a horse who has an issue with a certain fence, perseverance is key. I once had a young Thoroughbred off the track who I trained to jump. We soon discovered that a coop I had in the ring was going to be a problem. The jump was about 2'6" and it was shiny and this horse would not go near it. I could barely get him to pass between the coop and the rail, even though the gap was about 14 feet wide. If we tried approaching the coop to jump it, I couldn't get him within three strides. He'd run, panic, lose it. I just stayed at it. I kept riding him in the same routine, the same way. Pretty soon, I'd get within two strides. Then one stride. Then he'd canter right up to it like he was going to jump, and then stop and almost throw me off. Getting angry wouldn't work, so I just calmly kept at it, staying focused on what would get him to the other side. After three or four weeks of trying and ultimately still failing, I just continued to make the effort, no matter how difficult it was. But then one day, he cantered right down to it, jumped it, cantered away, and jumped the next jump out of the line. He never, ever looked at the coop again. I took him to a horse show and he never hesitated at a single jump on course. That's the example I think of when it comes to perseverance and patience (plus letting the horse think it's their idea), and how we keep trying no matter how tough something is." —CB

HOW ARE YOU JUMPING?

- How does your horse see the jump as he's approaching it? While they can see it from a distance, the horse actually cannot judge a jump anymore once he's about two steps away. So your job is to just continue to flow forward in the last few steps before takeoff.
- The landing of the jumps is just as important as any other part of the process. Think backwards from where you want to end up. So many people are fixated on riding to the jump that they only ride to the jump! They don't ride up and over the jumps and then away. Being hyper-focused on the jump itself—looking at the jump, thinking about the jump—this is a recipe for mistakes because it ends up making your balance low and encourages you to change your mind. All that thinking about the jump can lead to looking down at the jump, which always lowers your balance. But, if you think about riding your horse away from the jump for three strides, if you think "rhythm" and "straight" away from the jump, the jump itself will be better. Landings don't get discussed enough. Your landing is your approach to the next jump. So good landings make for good jumps.
- Always remember that you're not riding to the jump. You're riding to the jump, over the jump, and away from the jump. It's all one. The jump is not just the obstacle itself. The jump is the approach, the obstacle, and the landing. The quality

> "Ralph Caristo taught me that they used to jump only planks in the old days, not poles. They had big planks and there was enough depth to them that if the horse hit a plank, they would respect it more. A pole, they push out of the way. A plank turns in the jump cup. A pole rolls out, or if it's a squared pole, it's jammed in there. That's why, in my opinion, planks are safer." —CB

Riding away from the jump is just as important as your approach and the jump itself.

of the jump itself, the straightness, the balance, the organization—it's all going to be better when you think about the landing. When you're jumping out of a line, imagine that you have another jump four strides after the out. Your job is not done when you get out of the line.

- For a horse that stares and backs off at jumps, practice at home first over easy jumps, then begin slowly introducing anything that's new and strange—and safe to get to the other side. Hay bales, shavings bags, trees in the woods … but whatever it is, always have the horse land and gallop away more forward than they took off. Also have them comfortable on the other side. Horses are claustrophobic, so we always like to have them more open and free on the landing side until the horse starts to be confident going to the jump. For instance, don't have other jumps in their line of sight or close on the landing side. Approaching a jump systematically so the horse is comfortable and knows what to expect does help, but it's key to have them land more positively than they took off. Soon, you'll find they start to be more positive as they leave the ground.
- On a horse who's lost some heart at the jumps or lost their confidence for any

number of reasons, you want to give them confidence at every jump, even if you get there deep or long. Riding a horse like this, you want them to know that the distance that comes up doesn't matter. Every time they land, they are okay. You just canter away in a positive manner. This is helpful with all types of horses. Land and gallop away. Leave the jump behind your horse with more positive rhythm than you came in with. This builds confidence over time. Don't have a bad jump and stop. Continue on, jump a few more, so it's not a big deal.

- Another note on a horse that has to regain some confidence at the jumps: Think about incorporating gymnastics into your jumping. It doesn't even have to be an actual gymnastic, but you want to ride a jump with another obstacle to contend with next. You can set up a grid, or you can even just set a jump and then four strides to a cavaletti, and then three strides to another cavaletti. This way, you're always creating more positivity and going forward when you land. With repetition, the horse knows that they always need to land and go forward.

- For horses who want to rush the jumps, we try not to fight with them. We try to let everything be their idea. So, if the horse wants to run past the distance and chip, we don't force them to wait. We just ask for them to respond in keeping their pace and stride a bit longer. We don't try to overprotect them, because then it's the horse's idea. The next time they come around, if they're smart, they're going to back up, they're going to slow down. Using more solid jumps for this type of horse is helpful too, to naturally back them off a bit. You can train a fresh horse, but you don't want to teach a horse to get fast and flat. So we try to keep their focus. Canter around, work in some jumps, and then walk for a while, allowing them to take a deep breath. A fresh horse and a fast horse are two different things. Fast means a flat jumping style, whereas fresh doesn't always mean flat. We try to avoid flat at all costs.

- If you're jumping a hotter type of horse, you can also try incorporating descending height. If you're doing a gymnastic or a grid exercise, for example, it will encourage your horse to take a breath if you start with your bigger jumps (after a thorough warmup, of course) and then work your way down so that by the time you're done jumping, the jumps are very small.

- As for the rider's position over jumps, go back to where your body would be if you had no hands. Your leg would drop down, you'd have more weight in your stirrup, your core would engage, and you'd lift your eye and use your head for balance a bit. That's one of our favorite visuals. If you can't use your hands to balance on the horse's neck, you'd have no choice but to keep your body in a correct jumping position. A common mistake that riders make, especially those with less experience, is getting ahead of the motion in anticipation of the jump or asking the horse to jump by tipping forward. Visualize what it looks like when you allow the horse to jump up to you. Their shoulders are coming up and you have to create that space for them to lift. If your hands are in the withers and you're bending down over your hands, can your horse lift its shoulders? Picture the mechanics of the horse's jump: You want the horse to rock back, crouch a little, and the front end is going to lift up. Picture where you want to be during all those points of the jump. You're engaging your core and staying tall because you're allowing your horse to use their neck and back over the jump. Try visualizing it frame by frame to picture what your body needs to be doing to help your horse.

EXERCISES FOR JUMPING

- Try this exercise for sharpening your eye and knowing where you are: Start counting down to a single, small jump when you think you're twelve strides out. It doesn't matter how wrong you are! Just take that information and then go do it again, adjusting based on whether you were further or closer than you thought. Continue until you get it right, or stop and try again another day. As always, don't overdo it.
- We also like the circle exercise: Jumping a single, small jump on a circle numerous times in each direction. This helps you maintain a rhythm and use your track to fix the jump as needed by shaping your track in or out depending on how the jump is coming up. You can also add one or two more jumps on the circle. You'll see that different types of distances come up—some shorter and some longer—but any distance can be a good distance if you support it (more on this in Chapter 11).
- One method for perfecting your canter rhythm is to come up with a song that has the right rhythm for the canter you need while jumping a course. Maybe it's the Bee Gees' "Stayin' Alive," or even "Row, Row, Row Your Boat." You'll always work

> "Your shoulder should never get in front of the horse's shoulder over the jump. Most people get their chest over the shoulder." —CB

to maintain that canter rhythm to the song depending on how a horse responds to the jumps. While one horse sees a jump and wants to take you to it, another sees it and wants to step back. You're always adjusting to maintain your rhythm depending on what that individual horse needs. Having that song playing on a loop in your mind helps you to make the necessary adjustments. It can also help to keep you calm.

- In a lesson or at a horse show, don't take jump number one in your warm-up for granted. It's something trainers see all the time—the rider comes up to the first jump and the horse isn't paying attention, the rider isn't organized, and they fumble the first jump. Your first jump doesn't have to be perfect, but allowing jump one to be a throwaway is doing both you and your horse a disservice. No jump is a freebie. Your horse only has so many jumps in them, so make that first one count, out of respect for your partner. Train yourself to have a positive first jump, every time you are jumping. Prioritize it. It doesn't have to be perfect, just positive. It's so common: After a flubbed first jump, a rider will say, "I'd better get in gear!" Or, after a round at a horse show, a rider will come out and say, "After jump one, it was great." Training yourself to make that first jump a positive one is a game-changer. It's all about creating good habits. And, if you're not training/maintaining, then you're untraining, right? That applies both to you and to your horse. Don't take any jumps for granted.

> "When you're jumping a course, I like to say: You need to put some punctuation on it. Don't jump the course like a run-on sentence. Put a comma here, a period there, tap the brakes as needed. Build those punctuation, or 'reset' points into your course plan. Maybe you're jumping a single to a five stride line, and then you take a breath and reset. Add the period in there. Then move on to your next 'sentence' in the course." —TB

CHAPTER 11
"The Distance"

MORE THAN ANYTHING else while jumping, riders get fixated on and anxious about "finding the distance." Many trainers, ourselves included sometimes, will tell students that they shouldn't be looking for a distance so much as working to maintain their rhythm, pace, and track. An appropriate takeoff spot will almost always come up if you've got those three things. That said, having a visual cue can also prove incredibly effective, which is why we use a tool called The Box. More on this in a moment.

THREE TYPES OF DISTANCES

If you set your pace, establish and maintain your rhythm, and go straight, 98 percent of the time, you're going to get one of three jumps: an ideal medium distance, a little deep/close, or a little long/far. And then whatever you get, you focus on making it better. A chip can be a well-handled deep distance when you support your horse off the ground. If you've got a connection with your horse's mouth and your elbow's out in front of you, in those last few strides, you can sink in, bend your arm, and raise your eye. Your horse will compress and it will be a nice, slightly deep jump. Same with being a little long. You can relax your elbow over the last few strides, back it up with some leg, maybe a cluck, and allow the horse to open their stride over the last few steps in front of the jump. If the same thing keeps coming up for you—a little short or long—you'll need to adjust your track or your rhythm. Sometimes you need to adjust both.

THE BOX AND FOCAL POINTS

One of the teaching tools we use that works particularly well for visual learners is something called The Box. The idea is that, rather than riding to the jump and looking for a takeoff spot, you are riding to The Box. The Box is an imaginary rectangle on the ground in front of the jump, and the goal is to get your horse's front feet into that box for takeoff. You can actually draw the box in the footing when you're getting used to the concept—make the box about eight feet wide by three or four feet deep. Anywhere you place the horse's front feet inside the box will be a manageable distance. Riding to The Box teaches you to canter to any distance and find a way to support whatever you get.

The sweet spot would be for the horse's front feet to end up right in the middle of the box before takeoff, whereas if you place your horse's front feet toward the front of the box, you're going to be a little deep. If they're at the back of the box, you're going to be a little long. And of course, you don't want to be outside of the box in either direction. (The placement of the box will move based on the size of the jump because the arc of the horse's jump changes depending on the fence height. The smaller the jump, the closer you'll place the box to the base.)

> "When I was younger, I used to consistently chip in to the brush. It was explained to me visually, so I learned where horses left the ground for an ideal distance. It helped to draw a rectangular box at the base of a jump where the horse's front feet should be. If it's a comfortable distance, the horse's nose will always be on the front side of the jump before he takes off. My seat bones should be right around or just outside of the outermost line of the box. Most people ride too close to the jump. If you draw (and later just visualize) the box, you'll be amazed at how far off you can be and still be in the sweet spot for take-off." —CB

The key here is to keep your eye up rather than looking down at the box. You don't want to start looking for the box until you're about five or six strides away. It's more about knowing where the box is than actually looking at it. Don't dwell on it or get hyper-focused on the box. Just ride your rhythm and ride straight to that box. The box should become an image in your mind.

This brings up another common issue that riders face—where to look when you're jumping. We're careful not to say "look for the box." To some riders, that might imply looking down, which is never where you want to be looking. When your eyes are down, your balance is down (and forward). Try doing it on the ground. If you look down at your feet, your whole balance tips forward. Instead, you should be seeking the general area of the box, and letting the box come to you. And never try to decide too soon!

When you're far back from a jump, you can look directly at the box to get a sense of where it is, but then as you approach, you'll want to lift your eye and keep it up. You're trusting where the box is from that one quick glance. It ends up in your peripheral vision but you're not actually looking directly at it. When you're about five strides away, your eye needs to be up and focused on a point beyond, like the next jump. And then as you leave the ground, you raise your eye a little more.

You can also think about looking for what we like to call your landing lane. When you drive your car or ride your bike, you're not looking right in front of the hood or the front tires. You're looking down the road. Same idea on your horse. And you're looking with a little elevation by lifting your eye and even your chin. That's when things will come into focus. Your head weighs a lot! Looking down at the jump is detracting from the balance for both you and your horse.

People say to pick a focal point at the end of the arena or along a tree line, but if you're jumping two jumps, you can't keep the same focal point. It has to have two elevations in it—two jumps, two elevations, up and over. Then you get the lift and the roundness of the jump. If you stare straight ahead, the horse will be more inclined to just slide over the jump. Always think about the lift and train your eye as such.

A GOOD EYE

You hear a lot about riders having a good eye. It's an admirable quality that means a rider knows where they are and can find their distances well. However, what people often don't realize is that having a good eye can also make jumping more difficult.

When you have a good eye, you may have a tendency to decide too much, too soon. And that can lead to over-complicating or second guessing your decisions. Knowing you have that good eye can also put more pressure on you and your eye. When people first learn that they can see a distance well, they tend to plateau, or even go a little backward in their learning progression. Once they know they can see a distance, then they start really looking for it. And when you start looking too hard, or trying to decide too soon, you get in your own way, distracting from where your focus should really be—on maintaining your pace, rhythm, and track. When these setbacks do happen, we suggest going back to the basics of just riding straight, keeping a rhythm, and keeping a focal point, and the issue will resolve. Instead of getting attached to the distance or the outcome, trust that rhythm, pace, and straightness will get you there.

It can be harder if you've got a good eye to let the distance come to you, but that's the ultimate goal for any rider, no matter what sort of eye you think you have.

A long approach to a single jump is often the most difficult place on a course for riders because it challenges your ability to let the distance come to you. Riders can get to staring at a jump like this—almost looking at it too hard and making too many decisions. That's where you start trying to make a decision too far back, too soon, or changing your mind. All of this overcomplicates jumping a single jump.

The unsettled, restless monkey mind can get carried away with you on a long approach, wanting to make all sorts of changes. The jump is not a place

> "On those long approaches, sing a song to yourself, or go through that constant, scrolling checklist that's in your mind: 'Are my reins short enough? Is my eye level up? Am I around my horse?' You can be thinking about all those things until it's time to decide when you're leaving the ground, instead of changing your mind ten times. Tell yourself, 'It's not time to know yet.'" —TB

> "I've heard a lot about looking away for a moment on the way to a jump, but that doesn't work for me. Instead, if I'm starting to look too soon, I tell myself to exhale and I say to myself, 'Let the distance come to you.' That's my routine. And pretty soon, it shows up. Once I turn my head and look, I don't take my focus off the jump—I'm a preacher of that idea. There are so many techniques, but that's what works for me. And for many good students." —CB

to speed up or to start pulling on the reins. Staying focused on your checklist, and perhaps on counting your rhythm, "one, two, one, two," can help quiet the chatter.

Another fairly common habit among riders is to look at the top rail of a jump as their focal point, rather than looking beyond the jump. Plenty of riders are actually taught to do this. But the habit can absolutely be adjusted.

Like any other habit that you're trying to change, you have to do something new repeatedly, consciously, and consistently, over and over again. If your focal point is the top rail you want to retrain yourself to make your focal point a place beyond the jump, nothing but practice will get you there.

Changing a habit and implementing something new in its place takes time and repetition. It's about constantly reminding yourself, even if you mess up and revert back to your old habit. With time, it will get easier and you'll have to remind yourself less and less. But when you're changing your habits on horseback, you may always have to take inventory and remind yourself of the new habits you want to maintain. You can go over it each day before you ride. You can try keeping a note in your tack trunk or on your phone of three things you want to work on during each ride, and implement those new habits and goals with purpose.

> "I'm living proof that you can break this habit. I was taught to look at the top rail. And I missed all the distances. I buried my horses at the jumps." —CB

CHAPTER 12
Routines for Riding at Home

EVERYTHING YOU DO WITH YOUR HORSE at home sets you up for success (or lack thereof) in the show ring. Therefore, establishing routines to mold your horse at home, where he's comfortable, will ultimately pay off wherever you take him.

RIDE TO THE RIGHT

Have you ever noticed how many people get into the habit of starting off their ride tracking left? For that matter, why is everything with horses done from the left in the first place? In medieval times, knights wore their swords on the left because they were right handed, so mounting, leading, etc., was all done on the left, dating all the way back to those times.

Whether you're taking a lesson or just hacking, most people get on their horse and start to the left. It's almost automatic. But it can have lasting implications on the horses. It's easy to fall into the habit of always starting to the left but, luckily, it's also a fairly easy habit to break.

Because we are conditioned to do so much from the left, we suggest leading your horses from the right side often and making a conscious effort to turn them right. Horses do so much to the left that we want to balance them out and unwind them, even in the most basic scenarios like leading and turning. People turn horses left in the cross ties and into their stalls. So, of course, they develop muscles and coordination in that direction and on that side. We encourage everyone to switch this up. Start turning right some of the time! Most riders, when they first get on a horse, sit slightly to the left. That's because they got on from the left side. So after mounting, you have to actually reposition yourself slightly in order to sit straight.

Since horses turn right so little in their day-to-day movements, their muscle structure is not the same on both sides. Over time, the horse ends up less balanced, and perhaps less comfortable when they go to the right. At Balmoral, we make a point to spend all of December (all of our off-season and other times, too) turning our horses right, and we stay conscious about leading them from the right. Sometimes we even dismount to the right! This helps to even things out before our winter circuit showing. We may be extra aware of it for that month, but we don't only do it in December. That would

> "I often find myself riding on the incorrect diagonal, because I ride from outside to inside so much. If you use the inside diagonal you're pushing your horse to the outside rein. But if you consistently ride outside to inside, then it's all about evening out both sides." —CB

be like doing yoga for one month and expecting it to hold for the other eleven months! We just find that extra focus in December sets us up for a year of being as right/left balanced as we can.

Taking a month to switch things up and then carrying that practice into the new year is relatively simple. The difference-maker is when people actually take the time to do it consistently, so we encourage you to go this extra mile!

If for no other reason, consider where many horses have issues in the show ring: on the right lead, going away from the in-gate. That's where this right-side weakness will often show up. But making habitual changes at home, both on the ground and in the saddle, can add up to a significant difference.

You have to make yourself extra aware. In a lesson when it's time to start jumping, even we as trainers can become conditioned to say, "Let's canter a nice little warm up jump off the left." We have to stop ourselves and go, "No, let's canter off the right first." Change the sequence. Don't get in a rut. To take it even one step further, generally horse-shoers are right-handed, so that can affect the way they trim the feet, and the way the horse then travels. Because no person is symmetrical, right? So, when you've got an asymmetrical person shoeing a four-legged horse, what are the odds that the horse is going to be shod in perfect symmetry? Things like this in a show horse's life are cumulative, and if we think about it from the ground up, we can make a difference. But your whole team has to be on board with it, no matter the size of your team. Whether it's just you and your horse; or you,

"It's little things, repeated over time, that make a difference. It's not huge, difficult, intricate, or hard things. It's simple things thought out and repeated, over and over." —TB

"If it's your habit to start left, start to the right now. The next time you ride. Track right, left, right. Because horses prefer/are stronger on the left, riders often end up this way, too. It's an ongoing cycle." —TB

An example of cotton in a horse's ears

your assistant, your groom, your barn manager, etc., everybody has to be on board with the changes to help make your horse stronger to the right and more symmetrical. Everyone has to be observant.

DESENSITIZING TO PREPARE FOR SHOWING

Your stable's environment will provide other ways to desensitize your horse at home. One of our stables is actually in the city, and we have to walk down a street to get to the ring. It's like being at a horse show all the time. It's good and bad in that way, but it definitely desensitizes the horses, so that horse shows become no big deal to them. The more exposure your horse gets, especially if they're green or young, the less reactive they will become. We also find cotton in the ears at home (as well as at the horse show) to be helpful.

We always seem to have a dog near the ring. We have one at home, Violet Brooks, who will lie on the outside of the ring, and she knows not to be underfoot. It's all about getting horses used to different situations. If you're at a show and a dog runs in the ring, you don't get a re-ride. The horses might as well get used to a dog at the ring at home. But be *safe* when

Violet Brooks

you're introducing new things to your horses. We're obviously not encouraging loose dogs! You can safely and carefully acclimate your horse to different outside noises and activity.

PAUSE AT THE GATE

Another habit we practice religiously is that we never ride the horses straight back to the barn. We never want them to hurry home. Horses generally want to hurry home and they know where home is … the gate! This becomes another opportunity to establish good habits. After working, every horse in our program stands before he walks out through the gate, and pauses to take some breaths. No horse walks straight out, ever. We do it everywhere, at home and then we take the practice to the shows. It's ultimately a way to prevent a problem before it even occurs. You don't want the horses to go bolting back to the barn. You always want it to be a relaxed, easy transition from work in the ring to walking home.

A quick horse show aside: When we are riding our horses at a show, we also don't ride back to the barn on show days. They're led. On schooling days, we ride a long, indirect route back to the barn—no matter how late you are, or how big of a hurry you're in. You never go the route that's most direct. And we always ride the horses past the barn and then come back to it. As a result, the horse never hurries to the barn.

This habit extends to the warm-up ring, too, and we recommend always finishing at the far end of the ring, rather than stopping at the gate. Mix up where you stop, exit, enter, and dismount.

On a related note, always reduce before you stop. After jumping, maybe pop over a cavaletti or small vertical and then trot them down the long side, allowing them to stretch on a longer rein. Let them unwind if you can, especially if they're worried. Take this habit to the horse shows as well.

CONDITIONING YOUR ATHLETE

Riding at home always provides a chance to work on your horse's conditioning. It won't benefit your horse to come out and trot laps with their stride half as long as it should be, working at 20 percent capacity. We direct the young professionals who ride for us to really let the horses gallop, dare them to buck, blast it out, and then go back to the trot. Horses have to use all their parts at the gallop, and go through their entire range of motion while elevating their heart rate. To really gallop, horses need to use their back, their hind end, and their neck. By galloping a bit early in the ride, you free up their body and you loosen their muscles, and you let them get some energy out. It seems like it makes the horses happy, too. It gets them warm and gets their muscles and body functioning.

If you come out every day and just plod around at the trot for a while, you're not actually giving them a workout. They need to get their heart rate up and work that range of motion. Galloping is especially important for horses who don't get a lot of turnout. It's up to us to make those horses really use their bodies. This is paramount to fitness and conditioning.

Horses are athletes, like us. If you're running or riding an exercise bike and you're not sweating, you're doing something wrong. You've got to work your horses. Trotting and cantering around without really making the horse work is not a productive use of time. You will benefit the horse so much more by making shapes like circles or serpentines, get them moving off both legs, get them cantering through the middle, and galloping.

If you don't challenge the horse to go full force this way when they are exercising, they just kind of glaze over. And then you run the risk of them bucking you off the next day because you haven't truly put them to work! Or they could trip or land off a jump and stumble because their bodies are tight. Just because you've warmed up doesn't mean your horse is loose and ready to perform. Range of motion is big. You have to think: Is my horse going at 40 percent capacity or are they going at 85 percent? Are they using all of their parts correctly? That's an important piece of what helps horses to stay physically healthy. It gets the muscles warm, loose, and limber.

TAKE LESSONS WITH OTHERS

If it's possible within your program or through your trainer, we recommend riding in a group. While we personally teach both private and group lessons (and there's a time and a place for each!), we do see great value in group settings for lessons. It's extremely helpful not only to hear things repeatedly, but also to put that together with what it looks like in motion and in real time. When you ride in a group, you get to see what it looks like when someone gets it right, and what it looks like when they get it wrong. You get a visual. Ride along, see it, feel it for yourself. It's almost like getting an extra ride. At a horse show, you sit and you watch other people ride. So why wouldn't you take the opportunity to watch other people in your lesson doing the same exercise that you're doing? The shared experience also creates a bond and a fun atmosphere.

Taking group lessons can benefit the horses, too. Horses are generally better when they're in a group. You don't want to stop riding your horse alone entirely; he'll be alone when he competes over jumps. It all goes back to variety. Practice training at different times in the day as well in order to simulate showing at different times of day. Many horses get distracted at feeding time, so practice at that time on occasion.

BE ORIGINAL

When you're riding by yourself, try things out. If something isn't feeling quite right, try something different. Safely, of course, but just try things out. You want to get to a place with your horse where you can say, "Okay, that didn't work. Now I'm going to try it a new way." Don't fall into that rut of "This is the way we always have to do it because that's what I've been told."

And when you're not in the saddle, be inquisitive. Read. Watch videos. Learning never, ever stops when it comes to horses. Be curious. More on this in Chapter 17.

CHAPTER 13
Routines for the Horse Show

WE DO THINGS AT THE HORSE show much like we do them at home—and we recommend that you do the same! After all, the horse show is just a continuation of your training at home. Regardless of whether you are at home or away, the focus should be all about routine and expectation for the horses. We will also share some of our favorite horse show-specific strategies for helping the animals to adapt and perform at their best when it counts.

ARRIVAL AND SET UP

When you employ everyday strategies at home to benefit your horses' well-being, make those same adjustments at the horse show whenever possible, like modifying your show stalls to maximize comfort and safety. Refer back to Chapter 2 for the modifications we make to our horse show stalls. Placing hay mangers in the stall corners is a super important one for us, so we don't want the horses eating out of hay nets at our winter circuit when they're used to eating off the ground. It's more work up front to make those adjustments, but it will benefit the horses at the show and beyond.

LUNGING

Lunging at the horse show can be a good way to get your horses to stretch out and use their bodies when you're not riding them. But there's a whole lot that can go wrong as well. A horse going fast in a small circle is, frankly, a recipe for disaster. Too many horses get hurt lunging, so we recommend being extra careful with when and how you lunge.

When horses travel in small circles, cross-canter, or just go fast on the lunge line (often because they're scared), that's not training. Nor is it productive. Like everything else you do with a horse, *lunge with purpose*. We recommend extra-long lunge lines, and letting your horse jog or canter at the end of the line. We are never trying to get the horses to go fast.

> "If you watch horses in a field, sometimes they do cross-canter. This doesn't really tweak their body, unless you put weight on it by adding a rider. A horse is cross-cantering because of balance. When this happens on the lunge line, don't yank them in and stop them abruptly. Instead, gently slow the horse down and try again." –CB

If we bring a horse out on the lunge line and they happen to be fresh, we stop them. Instead of lunging in that instance, we might get on and canter them, in a controlled way, to get that extra energy out. We don't lunge to exhaust. We lunge to let the horse stretch and relax.

As a whole, people like to lunge a lot, and there are some key common mistakes. People tend to have their horses go to the left more often than not, particularly if the horse is a little wild. So they lunge to the left for a long time and then they maybe go right for a minute or two. Same thing in the warm-up ring with tracking left.

Therefore, we suggest lunging to the right, the left, and then the right again. For us, less is more when it comes to lunging. We use it only as a tool to loosen up the horse's body. When we do lunge, we prioritize lunging right and left, getting the horse to move in both directions equally. We also monitor the lunging ourselves, and take the time to educate our staff.

COPING WITH NERVES

For the majority of riders, anticipation is the most difficult part of competing. For many riders, actually getting into the ring provides a bit of relief because then you have something to do, not just something to think about ahead of time. Of course, for others, there's still a lot of nerves involved with those two minutes of ring time, so we'll cover strategies for coping with all the what-ifs as well.

When we talk through show day stress with some of our riders, they tell us they're nervous because they feel like everyone is watching them. To those riders, we like to say, "Nope. Nobody cares." And we mean that in the kindest, most helpful way ... everyone at the horse show is generally focused on themselves or their own students. So putting aside the idea that the whole horse show is watching you can be helpful in calming show nerves.

There is also no such thing as being perfect in our sport. You're partner-

> "The only way I have had any success is when I've approached things in a positive way. I'm nervous as heck every time I walk in the ring. I have the same issues as everyone else. It's all about how you deal with it. I put so much pressure on myself but, at the same time, the more I ride, the less pressure I feel." –CB

ing with a live animal, and every day is different. There are so many variables. You can have an excellent jump or a stellar course but that's not realistically something you can repeat over and over. So, the first step in relaxing horse show nerves is to let go of the need to be perfect—that's when the progress can really begin. You are striving for excellence. Not perfection.

Every show day, there can be a different goal. So instead of seeking perfection, we focus on each little milestone that we're trying to reach. Telling yourself "You've already done this" is helpful, too. We had one young rider who was having a really hard time and wouldn't even go in the ring at a show in the fall. Our goal at first was: Enter the ring. Everything beyond that is a bonus. By the end of the winter circuit, she would walk in smiling and laughing. That was huge.

PREPARATION

When you're going to compete, minimizing your nerves and maximizing your performance begins long before you even arrive at the horse show.

Start your preparations well before you're going to start showing. Get all your things together a few days in advance so you won't have to think about it on the day of the show. Make sure everything is clean and polished, your backpack or ring bag is fully packed, and that you get a good night's sleep. For younger competitors, parents should make sure kids get any pent-up energy out before going to sleep the night before a show. Everyone should also focus on nutrition and hydration before, during, and after competing. If you're not properly fueled and hydrated, you can't perform at your best. Eat breakfast and snacks as needed on a horse show morning, even if the butter-

> "Just showing up is brave. Just doing it is brave." —TB

> "Do golfers get a hole in one every day? Go easy on yourself. Set realistic and attainable goals. Then string those small goals together and, before you know it, you've come a long way." —TB

flies in your stomach try to tell you otherwise. In all areas, preparation is a big part of management.

Long before you're on your horse at the show, we suggest you learn your course and walk around the ring. (It's a pet peeve of ours when riders only learn the course while standing at the in-gate. How do you study for a test if you don't know the material?) Walk all the way around the ring if you can, and look at all the jumps from the angle at which you'll approach them. If it's possible, stand near the judge's box. Or, even better, stand in it if you're there early enough. Look at the ring the way the judge will, and see what the judge will see. Consider the slope of the ring, where you'll turn. Close your eyes and visualize your course.

For the horses, we usually get them out for a light ride on show morn-

> "I come up with three things I want to accomplish every round. Maybe it's to minimize the bulge, to get my horse back on the short sides, and to raise my eye level if I think he's going to peek at the oxer. Then I try to go out and just do those three things. Being specific this way helps to reduce the physical and mental angst." -CB

ings to stretch their bodies, not to tire them out. Then, when we get on to warm up right before the horse's class starts, it's just a little review. We don't do a lot of drilling in the schooling ring so that we can save our good jumps for the ring. We actually don't even call it the schooling ring—we call it the preparation ring! Once you get what you need, a few good jumps, it's time to show off in the ring and not waste your good jumps outside of it. Review and go! Be prompt to the ring.

As you're warming up, gallop in the schooling ring more than you'll need in the show ring. We like to tell riders to imagine what their horse's speedometer would say. For example, while they're galloping in the schooling ring, we'll tell them to gear up to 15 (or whatever theoretical speed makes sense in your mind), then take it down to 10, then back up to 12, and keep the 12. That's how you set your pace. Work the gears a little bit. You get a lot of pace, then you have just a little extra. Then you settle into a medium pace, you know what medium feels like, and you stay at medium. It's the same idea in the show ring. You can get a little above the pace, even if it's just in extra energy to get your horse up in front of your leg and filling in the reins, before settling into the rhythm you want to maintain. Ask yourself if your horse is pulling on one rein more than the other or leaning on one leg more and address that with your trainer as needed.

When it's time to go to the ring, we have students stand at the in-gate and just breathe deeply, even closing their eyes, as we picture and go through the whole course together. We visualize and talk about what it's going to feel like if they do everything correctly. Then, for some riders, it helps to hear a joke just before going in. For others, it can be helpful to walk into the ring pretending you've already had a mistake, and ride like you're just at home,

> "At shows, I walk around the whole ring in the morning, up high in the stands. Then I study the ground. I don't even care if the jumps are in the ring yet. I study the ground and the waves in the footing. That all makes a difference in how your horse goes. Growing up on a farm, you learn to study that. For example, if there's a swell in the ring for drainage, you're not going to ask for a lead change there. The terrain makes a big difference." –CB

CB up in the stands

training. Everyone is different, and part of a trainer's job is figuring out what works for each individual to maintain that mental strength and focus in the show ring.

As for the horses when we're at the in-gate, we let them stand for the whole trip before them to take a breath. The way the horse sees the ring—it looks like a pizza slice to them, or a piece of pie, and you're at the narrow end. If you stand a horse and face the ring, they will start to see it all as one area, even if there are jumps in it. We think it's a good way to get everyone in the right mindset before they walk in the ring. It's also part of the routine, which is centering for both horses and riders. Especially for those who get nervous. Having this routine and talking at the in-gate for a full trip is calming, to an extent. (Just don't let your horse fall asleep at the gate.)

Finally, it can be helpful to differentiate your horse's routine on the days that you are showing, rather than earlier in the week when you're training. Our horses know that we ride them to the ring on the days that we are training. But on days that they're showing, we always lead the horses to the ring. This requires more work and more manpower, but we want the horses to know that something special is happening that day. Our horses know that when they're being led to the ring, they're showing.

IN THE RING

We make our best choices when we're using our breath, so breathing on course is critical. Identify certain spots in the ring where you'll take a deep breath. The corners or the short sides often work well for that. Work it into

> "Never finish your time schooling in the ring at the end by the in-gate. You don't want them to be familiar with the in-gate. Especially from the inside looking out." —CB

Our horses are led to the ring, not ridden, on show days. This differentiates competition days from practice days at the horse show for the animal.

your course plan with your trainer. And as we've mentioned before, back up that deep breath with your leg while you're on course. You don't want your horse to mistake your big exhale as a sign that it's time to stop cantering!

When you enter the ring for an over fences class, a lot of people prefer trotting first, then coming down to a walk, and then picking up the canter. Some people (like CB!) prefer walking into the ring and striking the canter right from the walk. Whether you trot in your entrance or not comes down to whichever is best for your horse—whatever shows off their individual strengths. But either way, make sure your upward transition to the canter is

> "I take three deep breaths before I go in the ring, or even before schooling a horse, and everything goes much better. I inhale three times as deep and slow as I can, and then exhale the same way. The horse may do it too, which is great. Horses will usually hold their breath if you're holding your breath." –CB

direct, prompt, and with *purpose*. Do not wander around looking at all jumps. That seems to create a negative impression in most judges (like CB!).

Once you enter the ring for an over fences class, your top priority is finding and maintaining the proper pace and track on course. Most people start out cautious and, as they go around, they get stronger. Think about setting your pace before the first jump. The judge wants to see a positive first jump, not a tentative one. After that first jump, no matter how you got into it, step away, thinking about pushing the saddle out in front of you and moving the horse ahead of your leg. Start medium and stay medium instead of starting slow and increasing throughout. At the beginning of the course, maybe it's a press up to get to medium. After jump three or four, maybe you'll need to slow down a bit to get to medium. It should all match. As the course goes on, you can step down a gear or two if needed, and then encourage your horse to maintain that gear on their own. Practicing this a lot at home is a good idea so your horse expects it at a show.

When our riders finish a course in the show ring, we always have them canter halfway up the quarter line, past the first plane of jumps. Some horses learn to "count jumps," so to speak, and they'll sometimes anticipate the end of the course. (This can lead to unintentional trot jumps!) We always avoid pulling up near the gate, because we don't want to teach the horse that the gate means time to stop. Try cantering up the quarter line, usually past the first jump of a line, and then execute your downward transition before you start trotting, if possible.

After your trip, you and your trainer can review the performance and plan the next one. Did you communicate clearly what you wanted to the horse? Did you accomplish the three things you set out to do? How can you make the next trip more positive for the horse? If you have a mistake in the ring, we strongly suggest that you don't dwell on the negatives. We prefer to ask our riders, "What do we need to do to improve upon that last round?"

We also encourage all of our riders, especially during our winter circuit when we have multiple weeks, to do more than one week in succession. If a rider tells us they can do two weeks of the circuit, we'll strongly encourage them to do two in a row. It's another building block. The more you do it, the

> "Doing one horse show is doing one horse show. Doing two horse shows in a row is more like doing three horse shows. The more times in the ring in succession, the more you're going to improve. And it doesn't matter if you're doing the walk-trot or the Amateur-Owner Hunters. The sooner you do it, the more often you do it, the faster your progression builds." —TB

more you get comfortable, and the more you understand the system. Repetition builds skill, and you and your horse stay in the groove.

Finally, learn to capitalize on defeat in the show ring. It's not something people talk a whole lot about, but you can really start to grow from those moments of defeat. We all fail at things, possibly nine out of ten times, before we get it right. That's when you learn the most, during that process. So while it may feel like a failure in the moment, all those little failures are what add up to your eventual success. If a mistake happens in the show ring, capitalize on it, knowing that you are now one attempt closer to being successful.

A FINAL NOTE ON "THE SYSTEM" AT BALMORAL

Because we are systematic with how we run our program (with individual attention to detail, of course), we believe that it takes some of the stress off of our team and our riders by the time we get to the horse show. Routines can be just as helpful for people as they are for horses.

The system comes in handy for people who ride with us but don't live nearby, for example. Some riders don't get to practice a whole lot but they meet us at shows and will always be prepared. That puts them in a better position when they get on to practice at the show. Because they know our system. And the horse knows the system. This applies to groundwork, to riding—everything. You're not leaving anything to chance. Riders know what to expect and they know that their horse will be set up. You can do so much "riding" and preparation in your mind, watching videos, and visualizing, so that when it's time to ride at the show, you feel ready.

> "A horse show is a show, and a competition, but it's actually you against the course." –CB

CHAPTER 14
The Mental Game

SO MUCH OF RIDING IS MENTAL. And mental training, like any type of training, requires hard work. Being a good rider means being a good student. If you work hard at the basics and do your homework, you're going to be successful. We believe in the work ethic of riders more than anything. Natural talent for any sport will obviously help, but it's second to work ethic.

It's also helpful to know yourself, your strengths, weaknesses, and learning style. Are you a visual learner? Do you need an analogy? Do you need to feel something to understand it? Many trainers will pick up on what type of learner you are when you train with them. If needed, or if you're new to a program or trainer, tell them how you learn best.

SELF-TALK AND OCCUPYING YOUR MIND

Your self-talk in the saddle is absolutely key to working on your mental game. It's easy to tell yourself what you don't want—"Don't lean in," "Don't get ahead of him," "Don't look down"—but to be effective, you have to tell yourself what you do want. Flip the sentiment and make it positive. Your thoughts will ultimately translate into actions. *Don't* say *"don't!"*

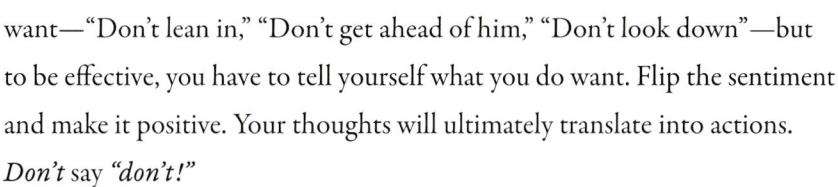

The *don't* is a negative. Frame it in the positive. Focus on what you need to do, not what you don't want to do. If you're concerned about your horse sucking back at the single oxer (either by his own choice or because you're getting stiff through your hands without realizing it), you have to think about the positive outcome. Tell yourself, "rhythm," or "maintain the pace," or "forward pace." That's how your brain tells your body to keep your horse continuing forward, rather than your brain telling your upper body and hands to take back. Sometimes you have to exaggerate these mantras, or repeat them more often.

An anxious mind is common among riders, and there are lots of ways to work on quieting anxiety and unhelpful mental chatter. One of our favorites is to count "one, two, one, two, one, two" to keep your rhythm as you're cantering around, particularly on the way to each jump, and for a few strides afterward. Sometimes you'll jump out of the "one" and sometimes the "two," but the more important thing is that you'll hear your rhythm by counting out loud or in your mind. The beauty of the "one, two" method is that it gives your brain something to do and a way to focus on your rhythm rather than anticipating a distance or over-thinking anything else that may be going on. Even just whispering or mouthing "one, two, one, two" keeps you breathing as well, which aids in staying calm. You can also sing a song, or do whatever helps you to keep your rhythm *and your breath*.

This is a tool you can take with you wherever you are riding. If counting or lip-synching helps quiet your mind so you can focus on your rhythm at home, do it at the horse show, too. Or lip sync. The judge will be happy to see that you're counting and doing something to maintain your rhythm on course. They are likely counting, too! We find that using one of these methods while in the show ring is especially helpful for someone who's nervous—which is about 95 percent of people at a horse show.

For other riders, counting backwards as you jump into a line can also slow down an anxious mind. Instead of counting, "Land, one, two, three, four, five," try reversing it. "Land, five, four, three, two, one." This is particularly useful if someone feels rushed to get out of the lines. You always want your horse to take his time jumping the oxer out of the line. But a rider's busy mind can result in a horse rushing out of the line—getting a little flat and just skimming over the oxer. Doing the correct number of strides and finding the distance are only the basics of jumping. At the next level in your riding, it's about how well you did all those things. Counting backwards is one of our favorite ways to get riders to slow down their minds while cantering down the lines.

Another common psych-out situation for riders is jumping downhill. Most rings aren't completely flat—they will have a grade, to some degree, so some

> "There are lots of little games you can play to train yourself not to take back and pull on the reins. Think about closing your hip angle and letting your elbows relax, exaggerating the motion as you count your rhythm. Counting calms your mind and gives you something to do. Count the canter rhythm 'one, two, one, two,' in your head while moving your arms to follow your horse. Tell yourself, 'I'm just cantering along, there's no jump here,' and maintain your rhythm. The jump just happens to be in the way. You cannot tell yourself, 'don't take back,' because then you're much more likely to take back. Instead, try saying something like, 'I'm just gonna flow until I know and it's time to go!'" –TB

jumps will ride uphill and others downhill. You may not even realize it at first. Even if it's only a slight grade, there's a visual and a mental sensation of traveling downhill, which can be unsettling.

In these downhill situations, try riding as if you're actually going uphill. It sounds overly simplistic, but it can make a real difference. To make a jump feel more uphill, all you have to do is raise your focal point. Think about riding up the escalator at the mall or in an airport. You don't look at your feet—you look up where you're headed. Think about that angle. As you're going downhill toward a jump, lift your focal point up a few feet. Your eyes are telling your brain and your horse where you're going. Use your imagination and make a little game of it. Once you've practiced making this focal point shift for some time, the downhill jumps won't feel truly downhill any more.

Walking around the ring at a horse show to assess the grade of the ring is helpful for visualizing how it will ride. Try it at home, too, and ride lines in both directions to see if you can feel the difference.

CHAPTER 15
Fear (a.k.a. The "F" Word)

EVERYONE FEELS AT LEAST a little anxious or nervous at times in our sport. It's completely normal. Even for professionals. But extreme levels of anxiety, or even fear, are important to notice and handle before they interfere with your ability to do your best with your horse.

It's easy to fall into the worry trap (what if … what if … what if ?) but the way we like to think about it is this: Worry is wishing for something that you don't want. You're giving it a lot of attention, increasing the likelihood that whatever you're worried about will actually happen. Instead, focus on the things you *do* want to happen (maybe re-read Chapter 14 about taking don't out of your vocabulary!). Control what you can control. When you're working through fear, over-preparing isn't the answer. Breathe. Take a walk.

One way to describe fear is the clever acronym False Experiences Appearing Real. To break down your feelings of fear, we suggest verbalizing what you're nervous about. What's the worst that could happen in any given scenario?

If it's falling off, tell yourself that it's happened before and, in most cases, you're going to be okay.

Another key question to ask yourself is this: Are you afraid of falling? Or of failing?

That's the first important determination you need to make. Is your fear physical or is it mental? Are you afraid of getting hurt or are you afraid of

> "You're allowed to feel afraid." —CB

doing something wrong? Breaking it down and talking it through with your trainer or fellow riders helps to dissipate the fear.

Once you've made that determination, say to yourself, either out loud or just in your mind, "THIS is what I sense." Then, just keep sensing it. Don't push it aside just yet. Really feel what you're feeling. Then let go of it. Take a breath in and then breathe it out of your system. When you exhale, feel the fear leaving your body, or pretend you're seeing it leave your body.

Hopefully it feels good to do that and wipes your mental slate clean. Then you can visualize your course and imagine what it would feel like if you were to score 100, or visualize what you're going to accomplish in your lesson at home. The fear doesn't disappear, of course, but you're pushing it to the back of your mind. We like to call that turning the fear away. It goes in the back. It doesn't get to be in the front! You're trusting in your trainer and your team—that they wouldn't put you in a position that you can't handle. So now the fear is in the back, and at the forefront is your visual of everything going exactly the way you plan.

Everyone copes with fear differently. With some people, we try to fill their minds with what they need to think about, while with others, we tell jokes or distract them a little. We can also help to channel that nervous energy into excitement. Flip the script and tell yourself you're excited, rather than nervous. You can use your adrenaline and channel it into rising to a challenge. Reframe it. It's individual and unique, but find what works for you.

> "I embrace going into the ring a little nervous and afraid. Accidents happen when you don't have that adrenaline. You have to be a little nervous—that goes into any athlete who's trying to perform. Embrace the fear factor and capitalize on it." –CB

It can also help to use the strategy from page 121 about identifying three things that you'll do in any given trip. Breaking it down to specifics and focusing on just three small goals will leave your mind less room to wander and worry. We find that for a lot of people, it helps to make one of those three things simply, "I will do the best job I can for my horse." We get so stuck inside our own heads that it can be beneficial to turn your attention to your partner and what you're going to create for them in the ring.

Be specific in identifying what you can control. Say you're concerned about the brush jump. You can make one of your three things: "I will let my horse get to the brush in front of me." Notice that we did not say "I won't lean up at the brush." That goes back to the idea that your thoughts create your actions. When you're identifying your three goals for each trip, always think about what you do want to achieve, not what you're trying to avoid. Frame it in the positive.

At the end of the day, sometimes people need to learn things in a pressure situation. Making a mistake in the show ring is different from making a mistake at home. You'll likely be pleasantly surprised by how much you'll learn the more you show. Just stay open to all the teaching moments as much as you do the victories.

FEAR OUTSIDE THE SHOW RING

We give so much credit to people who start riding as adults. Even if you rode as a child and stopped for a while and started back up, that's still much more of a foundation than starting from scratch as an adult. Everyone who began riding in childhood knows that the fear factor is completely different as you

> "Leslie Steele often says, 'Nerves are good. Nerves mean you care.' That is something I repeat often." —TB

age. You grow up, you have responsibilities, you understand your own mortality, and suddenly there's a fear element to riding that wasn't there before.

But fear doesn't just strike in older riders or beginners. Fear comes in to play for advanced riders and even professionals, too. It truly happens to everyone. A lapse in confidence is something that happens to athletes in any sport—golfers, baseball players, race car drivers, whomever.

Learning how to fall is one exercise that can help both your confidence and your ability to control what happens in the event you come away from your horse, which we all know is inevitable. We have often used a bucking barrel, which is suspended a few feet above the (padded) ground by ropes to let riders safely practice falling. As they're rocking around on the barrel, we say, "You pick when." Because we want people to realize when they're going to fall off and pick a spot to land. Of course, you don't always have a choice, but it's good to be prepared for the times that you do.

As trainers, our job description involves being part psychologist for our riders. A good trainer is going to have empathy for their students. Just as everyone learns differently, everyone processes fear differently. Having a trainer who will treat you with kindness and empathy during struggles with fear (or anything else) is important. Do you need a stern push, or do you need a supportive listener? There are different approaches for different riders. A good trainer will learn what you need once they've gotten to know you.

There are also different kinds of fear—based on different origins. There's the type of fear typically found after someone has had a bad fall or another bad experience. There's the fear of the unknown. There's the fear of being out of control. And on top of these origins, you have to consider that some people's makeup is simply more anxious than others.

So how do you combat the fear on a day-to-day basis? We always try to break it into pieces to help people feel like they're in control and feel secure in the saddle. We do a lot of exercises around that, a lot of practicing the basics, and we recommend that you do the same, no matter what level you may be. Even with the riders who compete over higher jumps, we don't routinely jump big jumps at home.

We do a lot of technical things at home at a low height. It's easier on the horses, and it's easier on the people. We also try to not throw too much at them at once. We do it in building blocks—we try to master one thing, and then move on to the next, so that riders aren't thinking about too many things at once. When you practice your basics enough, they become such a regular part of your ride that you don't have to concentrate on things like keeping your heels down or keeping your eyes up.

We have one rider who's struggled a lot with fear. And recently, she was trotting over a little jump and the horse caught its toe and stumbled. Before, she would have pulled up right away or she would have just frozen. But after the work we'd put in, she was able to just keep going and do it again, preventing her from dwelling on it. Remember: The best way to get out of trouble on

> "Going too slow is actually scarier than going forward. Timid or fearful riders want to be cautious—so, naturally, they want to go slower. But if a horse isn't going forward, they won't have enough momentum or power to get themselves out of trouble if a mistake were to happen. I try to explain to fearful riders that they can actually get into more trouble by going too slow than by carrying some pace. Pace helps your horse to help you!" –TB

a horse—to get through anything in riding, really—is to go in a forward direction. Forward is your friend! If your bike is about to fall, you pedal faster. You go forward to get through it. If your horse starts to stumble, you're not going to pull on the reins or stop. You're going to put your leg on and move the horse forward, away from the problem. Don't let one problem turn into ten!

Being positive on a horse means going forward. We train our horses to understand that it's always about going forward. We try to make it instructive for our riders, too. An important part of your job is to make things comfortable for the horse. That means not dwelling so much on your own fear.

Because it's not just about you. It's about the horse, too.

*Note: *It can be helpful to seek the help of a sports psychologist (ideally one who focuses specifically on riding). This is particularly beneficial if you feel like fear is getting in the way of your productivity and your enjoyment of riding.*

CHAPTER 16
Laugh at Yourself —CB

PLAIN AND SIMPLE: You have to be able to laugh at yourself. If I make a mistake, I laugh first so everyone laughs with me.

For a long time, whenever I would make a mistake, I would get very embarrassed. I'm shy by nature, so I would go off alone and beat myself up. I thought everybody was looking at me, laughing at me. I felt very humiliated.

Then I learned, unfortunately later in life (I wish I'd learned it sooner), that I can find humor in myself, and not take myself so seriously, because everyone else is looking for humor too. If you can actually laugh at yourself, other people will enjoy the humor and laugh with you, not at you.

One of the best things I've learned in my life is about how to deal with myself. If I make a mistake when I'm training or competing, when I see that I'm making that error, I start to laugh about it. Yes, I work at solving the problem, but I don't get tense and tight. You've got to be able to enjoy yourself, even when things aren't perfect. You've got to be able to laugh at yourself. You are your own best friend.

I'll give you another example. At one winter circuit, I'd come to a combination and the horse stopped, very suddenly, and shot me into the jump like I was a bullet shot out of a gun. I got up, my face was bashed in. I led the horse out of the ring and said, "I'm too old for this. Why me? This shouldn't be happening." And then I took a minute and I realized, "You did this and you should've

Sleepwalk and Carleton in Harrisburg

done that." So, I got back on, jumped a jump in the schooling area, gave the horse some confidence, walked back in the ring, and won the class. But I laughed at myself and told myself what I'd done wasn't very smart. If I couldn't have laughed at myself, that horse probably wouldn't be competing any longer.

Humor about yourself goes extremely far. Anytime you get intimidated, you've made a mistake, or you've been rejected, try to find some humor in it and laugh at yourself. I truly believe that in order to get something accomplished, you might fail nine out of ten times. I know I do. Sometimes I'll get to about the sixth failure and think, "I've only got three more to go! I'm gonna get this." I laugh at myself. And you know what? My life's been much better ever since.

I'll leave you with one of the most memorable times I was left with no choice but to laugh at myself. We had a horse named Sleepwalk for a new owner, and I was showing him in Harrisburg back in 2001. Since it was around Halloween, they had a lot of pumpkins lined up on the rail as decorations. The ring at Harrisburg also has those leaderboards on the wall where they list the leading hunter and jumper riders over the years. We finished our course and it was very good, a lot of people were clapping, and I went to make my finishing circle. We got to those pumpkins, the horse spooked, and I fell off and hit the wall—right where I was listed as the leading hunter rider from 1996! I slid down that leaderboard on the wall like Wile E. Coyote hitting a cliff.

I was angry at myself in the moment, and then I laughed. Everyone else was laughing, so I didn't have much choice! We joked about drawing a chalk outline of a body, like the cops do, on the wall. Later that year, the judges told me they had me on top before that, too. I laugh about that story every year now.

CHAPTER 17
Learning Out of the Saddle

DURING THE TIMES that you can't actually ride, there are still plenty of opportunities for learning. You've got a nearly endless supply of books, magazines, blogs, and other media to consume, but one of our very favorite suggestions for riders is to watch videos or other people at the horse show.

Actually, we suggest you ride along with videos or the riders at the show. Allow us to explain.

Sure, you can learn a lot by passively watching others ride. But we recommend taking it a step further and "riding" along with the actual rider. Imagine what it would feel like to be on that horse, in that moment, and "ride" the course along with the rider. You'll get a lot more out of it than just passively watching. It's a lot more fun, too. And don't just watch the good rounds. Watch the mistakes, too. See if you can identify what happened and why. This is great education and there's an endless supply!

There are also lessons to be learned from watching what goes on at the barn, from the work of the barn manager, to the grooms, the vet, the farrier, the chiropractor—you name it. In many situations it's preferable to sit back and watch without interrupting, but in some circumstances, professionals do welcome questions from horsemen who want to learn more. Typically after they're done working, of course. Understanding how horses move and think can only improve your riding.

Funny as it may sound, there's an element of osmosis at play, too, when you're taking in things around the barn. Be there: Observe. Absorb. If you're just present and you let yourself be in the moment, you're going to absorb a lot without even having to ask questions. Put your phone down when you're at the barn in order to really soak it all in. You might not realize it at the time, but knowledge is seeping in.

THE TRAINER-CLIENT RELATIONSHIP

Any good trainer is going to try to do what's best for you and your horse. And you want to be involved, of course. But to get the most out of the trainer and client relationship, like any relationship, there is a time for listening, and a time for questions and conversation. Timing is everything!

Trainers work to do the best they can for you and your horse, and it's a process. Think about yourself as a student of this sport and not a customer or a client who is comparison shopping. Riders can innocently interrupt or impede a trainer's process, slowing it down. That can be the case with the parents, too. It's all about developing the relationship and feeling out what works best for your particular trainer with questions and conversations.

> "I think anybody who really wants to understand the whole industry and sport will take every opportunity there is to watch and listen. But I always try to stand back out of the way while other professionals are working." —CB

As trainers, we give our full attention to the horse and rider in front of us, but then we can pretty quickly move on to the next lesson, the horse show, or whatever is happening next in the day. Being upfront when you have questions or you want to have an in-depth conversation keeps everyone on the same page, and your trainer can schedule a time to have that talk when you'll get their full attention. Know that your trainer likely has (or should have) a plan and a reason for everything, even if they don't have time for an in-depth explanation at a given moment. Trust is huge. You hired an expert—trust them to do their job! They've seen this movie many times.

Each trainer's communication style is different as well. Some are great communicators and others aren't. It's that simple. And the client-trainer relationship is like any other relationship in that it has to be a good fit between your communication styles. You have to understand each other to a degree. Part of being a good client is about learning the trainer's communication style and personality and deciding whether that's a good match for you.

In our program, we take the reins quite a bit when it comes to decisions on vet, farrier, and other services. Our clients trust us to make those calls without always asking permission. But we never abuse that, and if there's a conversation to be had, we make sure that happens. Each program will be different in that regard. It's up to you, as the client, to decide whether the communication and decision-making style of a particular program works for you.

We also think it's interesting to note how often goals change for a rider. We have so many people come to us and say they want to ride, but they have no interest in showing. "I never want to compete." We hear that a lot. But then what happens is, after taking lessons for a while, people want to see where they are in their progress, and what they need to work on. They realize that horse showing isn't about competing with other people so much as competing with themselves.

That's the fun of showing, after all—seeing how much better you've become and what you need to work on when you go back home. Having those two minutes in the ring where your trainer can't talk to you and you have to think for yourself and make those adjustments and decisions. It's not so much "I want to compete." It's more that you've done all this studying … and then at some point, you want to take the test. It's not about the competition or winning ribbons. It's a way to see all that you've learned and what you need to work on to keep improving. You can't replicate the feeling of being at a show at home. Give it a try with the right attitude!

THE TRAINER-PARENT RELATIONSHIP

This relationship is going to look different than that of a trainer and an adult rider. It's so important for a child rider to be responsible and accountable while being focused on their trainer at the barn. We don't want them always looking to their parents. For a trainer-child rider relationship to flourish, there has to be trust and a little independence. Parents want to help, and they want to be involved. And that's great, but there does need to be space for the child's relationship with the trainer outside of mom or dad. For us, this is where we see a lot of growth amongst our younger students. For many young riders, a strong bond is formed and they look up to and trust their trainer.

Sometimes parents have lots of questions about the training their child is receiving. While the trainer, child, and parent should always be on the same page regarding goals and expectations, this is also an opportunity for the rider

Traci with Claire Van Konynenburg, mother of then-junior rider Kaitlyn Van Konynenburg.

A young rider gets prepared to go into the show ring.

to deepen their understanding. We encourage our child riders to explain what they're working on to their parents. Being able to verbalize what you're doing is helpful for any rider, so this is a way for parents to get involved that benefits the child's riding education. If you can talk about it, you can picture it. And picturing what you want to do in your riding is a big step toward being able to execute.

If a young rider has concerns or starts asking their parent a lot of riding questions, we ask the parents to please refer the child back to us. It's so important that a child rider feels comfortable speaking with their trainers about any questions or concerns. And if they're not, that means we need to work on that relationship.

One of the most helpful things a parent can do is prioritizing the relationship between their child and the child's trainer. We want young riders to feel that they're in charge of their riding journey. And when the parent feels their child is old enough, we encourage them to drop their son or daughter off at the barn for their lesson. It goes a long way when a young rider feels like horses are their thing. They own it, and that breeds confidence.

Parents, please remember that the trainer is training your child, not you. Please don't detract from your child's learning time. While riding is their thing, try to educate yourself by watching and listening. Time your questions carefully and make a point of not being around sometimes.

In a lesson or at a horse show, we want a child to be 100 percent focused on their animal and their trainer's instructions. We encourage parents who want to watch to do so from an unobtrusive spot. The best way to support your child's riding is to be supportive but not distracting. A parent's support can sometimes feel, to the child, like expectation or pressure. We also share a one-page document with new horse show parents that explains our protocols and procedures for the horse show.

A parent not familiar with riding may not realize that they shouldn't come over to congratulate the child after their first course since the child will be learning the second course. Part of educating child riders is also educating their parents. Watching from the in-gate would be like coming backstage before a child's performance. It's a distraction that detracts from the performance, so we advise parents to stand elsewhere while they're watching at a show. We know how much parents want to support their children, so we try to help them understand the best way to do that around horses.

We also want to make sure that parents realize that they can't compare their child's experience to another child's experience. It's understandable to look at other children in a program and wonder why they are moving up a division and your child is not. If your child is working with a trainer you trust, you can feel secure knowing that they are working on your child's timeline. Trainers want to help every rider meet their goals, but that journey is not the same for everyone. There are many paths to the end goal. Each path and experience is unique.

On the next page, we've included an abridged version of the document we share with new horse show parents at Balmoral. While some of it is specific to our program, we hope that much of it can be helpful to new horse show parents everywhere.

BALMORAL
General Guidelines for Horse Shows

Our staff will contact you with an overview of the schedule and the location of our barn/stalls. The evening before show days, look online to check your show times. Please plan to arrive at least an hour before you show. For schooling days, please let us know in advance your day and time of arrival so that we may plan lessons, horse work schedule, etc.

ARRIVAL Please head to the barn to touch base, grab whatever you need from your trunk, and check in. Riders should arrive dressed to show or lesson (breeches, boots—clean and shined, hair pulled back/braided, belt, etc.). Older children should check their ring and start to learn their first course and do their walk around. You will usually find us at the rings if we are not at the barn.

SHOW TIMES Please keep in mind that horse show schedules are not set in stone and times/rings may change. We will let you know when you need to be at the ring to show. Each night, the shows post time estimates online for the following day. This is our only guide to give you a window for show times.

Times are based upon how many riders are entered in the classes preceding yours. We have no way of knowing this (beyond estimating) until the show posts it. Best to plan to be at the show most of the day as far as scheduling other activities for that day.

BARN Please do not feed treats in the cross ties, as this gets all of the horses excited and makes it difficult for the grooms. You are welcome to leave treats in your horse's stall. Please keep your personal items in your tack trunk (with lid closed) or hung up in the dressing room area. Please help yourself to bottled water & snacks in the dressing room.

IN-GATE & SCHOOLING RING Please stay clear of the in-gate at all times. The in-gate area is for competitors and staff only. This area is congested and can be dangerous for spectators or extra people; it is an area for professionals and riders only. It is not an area for family/friends/dogs to congregate, as it is dangerous and they can distract riders who are trying to learn courses and focus before they compete. Only trainers, grooms and competitors should be near the in-gate. Sometimes classes run back-to-back which means riders have a small window of time to learn their next course; they need to stay focused. Words of encouragement should be given before your child gets on the horse and not at the in-gate. Our staff will offer water before and between rounds. Once your child has completed showing and discussed it with their trainer, they will dismount and head over to you.

UNFORSEEN CIRCUMSTANCES Falls happen. If your child falls off, please remain calm and DO NOT enter the ring, unless your trainer calls for you. Most often riders get up, brush themselves off and get back on. Because this is part of riding, we try not to dramatize it, and we keep moving forward.

DEPARTURE Please touch base with our staff before leaving the show so we can give you an estimated arrival time and any pertinent information/plans for the next day.

QUESTIONS Please know that each rider/horse/situation is unique. Just because your child/horse requires/does something, doesn't mean that someone else's experience is the same. If you have questions, please feel free to ask our staff at a time when they are not busy (or at a scheduled time), and understand that other parents may not know the answers. Please know that although parents might be trying to help, they may not have the answers for your specific situation.

> "Every moment of success I have achieved, I have shared. I must thank the thousands of horses who have helped me develop into the person—and just as importantly, the horseman—that I have become." —CB

LEARNING FROM YOUR FELLOW HORSEMEN

Those who know Carleton know that he's got two ever-present accessories: an orange baseball cap, and a notepad that he carries wherever he goes. A most diligent student, he is constantly taking notes. And that's because every single day brings opportunities to learn, and people bring those opportunities with them.

It's funny how many things you think you've figured out on your own while working with horses—and then you find that someone else has been doing that very thing forever. We once found an article about a man starting horses in a hackamore and that's something we've often done, too. It was great reassurance to see that parallel.

The difference-maker, when it comes to knowledge, is whether you're really going to use it and incorporate it into your own work with horses. People can be greedy when it comes to knowledge, just grabbing it so that they have it. There can be a "the more, the better" mentality. But we can't read a book for anyone else—you have to read it yourself. We encourage all horsemen to not only acquire knowledge wherever you can, but to use it and apply it to your specific animal however that works best.

We also learn from our horses as much as we do from other people. With each horse in our barn, whether it's an investment animal, a client's horse, or a sale horse, we hone in on what they, as individuals, have to teach us. And we almost always learn something from each horse that will ultimately help us with another horse.

> "Ask for help, get all the good advice you can, and then distill it into what works for your situation." —TB

Nick Haness (left) riding for Balmoral, and Carleton conferring with Tori Colvin.

It's the same way with other trainers. We are not afraid to call other professionals. You cannot be afraid to ask other people at the top of your game for help. We also wouldn't hesitate to ask questions of someone in the Western world or another discipline if it might help us over here in our hunter jumper world. You cannot limit yourself when it comes to the knowledge you can share with others. You see something and you go, "Oh, I could use that." And then someone comes to you and says, "I am having trouble getting this horse to do such and such." And then it's our turn to say, "Well, we do it this way." This exchange of information, it's all about continuing to move forward. Just as it is when you're riding. Keep moving forward. More and more brain power. Be generous with knowledge and open to receiving it. There's never just one way to do things.

An integral part of why we consider ourselves horsemen is because we do not just go with one train of thought and decide, "Okay, that is it. That is how we do things." It's all about having an open mind and being receptive to different ideas and ways of doing things. It's not about taking the first answer you're given so much as collecting different answers and seeing what works with each individual horse. And this takes time and effort. *Patience = progress.*

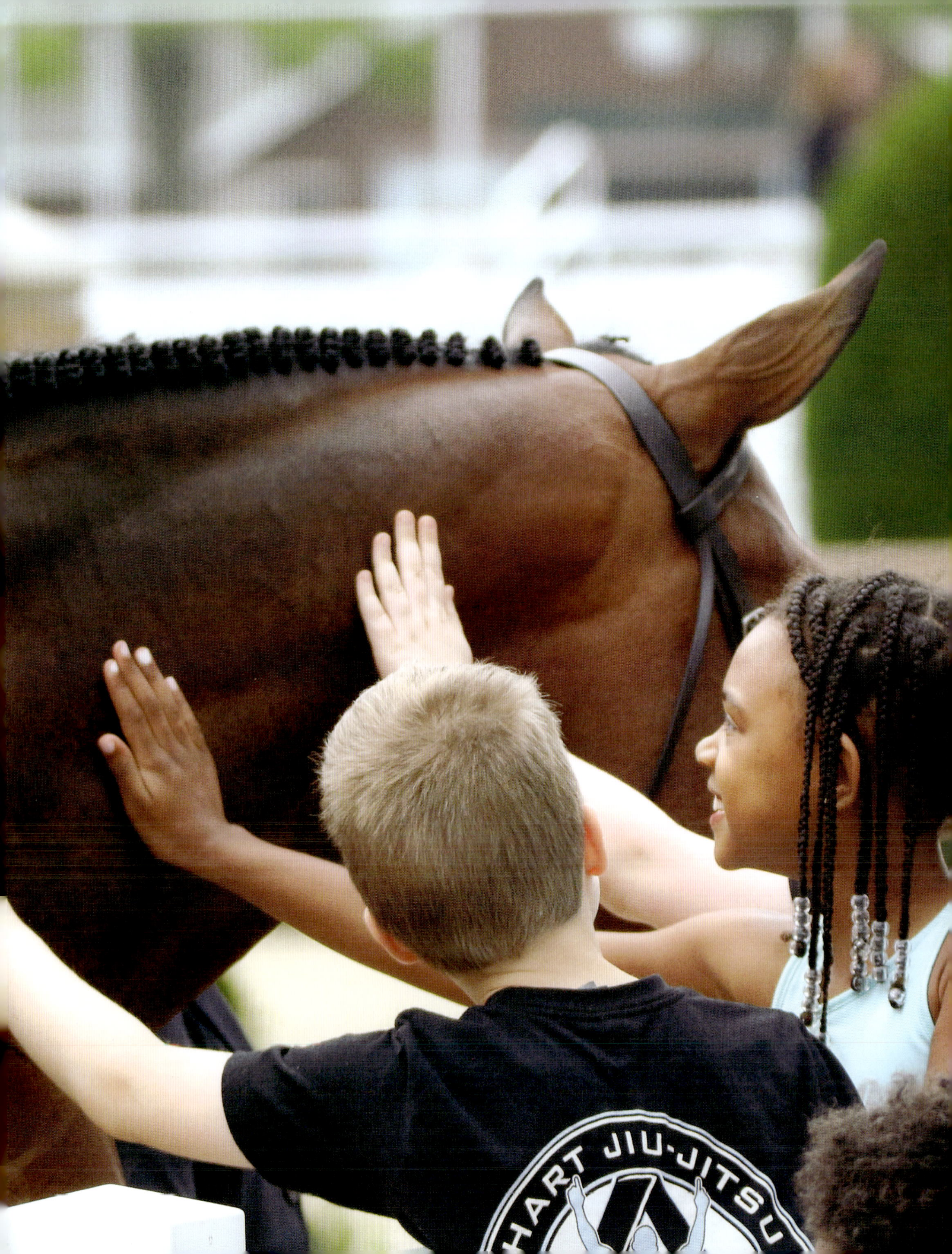
HART JIU-JITSU

PART III
On the Industry

AS PROFESSIONALS, it can be easy to get fixated on the business of the horse world. But when something happens to remind you of the simple enchantment of horses, you appreciate it. And share it.

Around 2014 or 2015, we were at the Devon Horse Show outside of Philadelphia. Devon is a prestigious event more than a century old that's steeped in tradition—a big local and national spectator event. All day long, there are spectators walking through the barns, just wanting to get a glimpse of the horses behind the scenes.

One day, a mom with her little girl, who was probably three or four years old, came walking through. We said hello, gave them a carrot to drop in a horse's feed bucket, and off they went.

That night, the horse show ended late, as it can do, and we went to dinner. We were in a rush so we sat at the bar at our favorite restaurant. As we chatted with the bartender, we realized that she was the mom who came through earlier that day. She told us that they live nearby and look forward to this event every year—and how much her daughter loves the horses. Her daughter was specifically drawn to our horse Triton Z. We invited her back to visit the next day ... and the day after, and the day after. This little girl got to spend time with Triton and our head groom, David, who let her sit on Triton in the stall. The girl got to see him show with his rider Kaitlyn, and clap with us at the end of their rounds.

Every year since then, just before Devon, we touch base with them, confirm that we'll be at Devon, and make plans to see each other. This little girl has become our helper, assistant, cheerleader, and good luck charm.

The two have since gotten a horse of their own. They keep the horse at a local barn and do the care themselves.

That's what it's all about when you work in this industry, isn't it? We are all bonded by a shared love for horses, and we take great pride in opening up our world to those outside it. Part of our job is welcoming people to love horses alongside us.

152 ♋ WITH PURPOSE: THE BALMORAL STANDARD

CHAPTER 18

Barn Culture

GROWING UP WITH HORSES

PART OF WHAT'S great about growing up at the barn is that everybody's there for the same reason—because they love horses. You can be eight years old, or fifty-eight years old, but you're there together with a shared passion and understanding, and the age kind of melts away. The older riders help the younger ones, and the younger ones aren't intimidated by the older ones. They look up to them, and then, when they go out into the world or they go to school, it gives them so much more confidence in dealing with all kinds of people and situations.

Parents notice a difference in their children's happiness and confidence when their children ride. There's something about children being able to relate to this big animal, feeling like they're good at something, and feeling like they're on equal ground with older kids.

Plus, it just gets more fun the more time you dedicate to this sport. Learning to post is hard, but once you've mastered that, trotting is a lot more enjoyable. Once you learn to canter, it's even more fun. We tell beginners to just hang in there through the beginning because it gets more and more fun as you learn. And the time you spend pays off! They feel the progress and they're empowered.

We also find that the processes around riding lessons are beneficial for kids. Children want to know what's expected of them. And those rules are naturally built in when you're taking lessons. The kids know: I need to be early to be on time. I don't come to the ring with dirty boots. I don't come to the ring with my hair hanging out, or my shirt untucked. I always wear a belt. It's regimented. We think that on some level, whether they realize it or not, children appreciate structure (we know that horses do, too!). Especially when it's not coming from their parents.

Having a routine and knowing what's expected also gives kids security. There are no surprises. They learn the way to take the pony to the ring, they ride the pony, then they need to put the pony away, take their saddle, clean their bridle. They don't just walk away, and they don't just get to come and ride. They have to do all the other stuff, too—they have to earn the riding. And then we'll see them cleaning their bridles, chatting and goofing around. It's like the water cooler. They're just standing around and telling stories. "I finally got five strides down the line today." Or, "My pony was wild today." It's good. You can see them decompress and connect.

HANDS-ON LEARNING

Anytime we can, we want our riders to be hands-on with their horses, and we suggest the same for every rider out there. The hands-on time is part of what elevates you from a rider to a true horseman.

This will vary depending on the program you ride in—some are more self-service and others more full-service. We are generally a full-service program, but for people who are just learning, we prioritize having them tack, untack, and groom whenever possible. We'll have camps in the summer, and sometimes over spring break or Christmas break. If it's raining, we'll have a horsemanship day where kids will come in and their bridle will be in pieces, and they have to put it back together. We make it a game.

Sometimes we'll conduct a quiz on horse anatomy and whoever knows the most answers gets a prize, like getting to ride bareback or another fun activity with the horses. Some of the kids enjoy this part more than others. But there are plenty who do love it, and who would spend the whole day pushing the wheelbarrow and grooming horses if you let them. It's always refreshing to meet kids like that. Helping a child to understand horses from the ground creates a foundation for understanding riding.

We try to instill in them that it's the entire process that matters—getting to know your horse and creating that relationship from the ground up. Does the horse have a bump on its leg that wasn't there yesterday? Does the horse like it when you use the curry comb or the softer curry gloves? All of those things contribute to the horse and rider bond. We tell our riders, "Do you think we figured out all this stuff just by riding? No. You have to spend this time with your horse on the ground. The riding is a small part. If you love your horse, you need to be taking care of them, or at least know how to do so. Riding the horse is not taking care of the horse. Riding the horse is taking care of *you*."

We also tell budding horsemen and people new to the sport that feeding your horse, making sure they're healthy and clean—these are things the animals can't do for themselves. You have to be in charge if you really love your animal. We can be pretty firm with young riders and, generally, the parents like that (the discipline and work ethic crosses over into other aspects of the kids' lives). A level of discipline is an integral part of the riding experience.

It's important, after all, that kids pay attention any time they are on or around these big animals, and that they aren't distracting other kids in or around the lesson. We'll say, "If you're not focused, or if you're not paying attention, that's not safe and your lesson will be over." You ask your horse or pony for 100 percent, so you need to give them 100 percent of your attention.

Being a good horseman and a good student is inextricably linked with being a good rider, and that's something we try to instill in all our riders, young and old.

HORSES MAKE NICE PEOPLE

When kids learn to take care of animals, it makes them kinder, more empathetic, and more responsible people. There are so many ways that children benefit from learning horsemanship and how to ride. But this applies to adults, too. The end goal of being with horses, in the big picture, is bigger than riding and showing. Ribbons aren't the end goal. Riding and working with horses is like a metaphor for life. You're going to face some adversity—how do you approach it? What are your coping mechanisms?

It's about being self-aware. If you know you get a little bit of anxiety around X, Y, and Z, how do you deal with that? We think that's a big reason why adults ride. They get to know themselves and how they're wired, how they operate and what they need to do to improve themselves. That's a big part of the challenge in riding—and in life. There are so many parallels.

Consider a nervous adult rider who keeps showing up. She's not going to be attached to the outcome, and she knows how good this sport is for her life, so she just keeps coming back. It doesn't get much better than that. What horses do for people—well beyond the ring—is an integral part of our philosophy.

CHAPTER 19

Our History with Horses

CB: I started out riding in the cornfields near my childhood home in Indiana. Our first two horses were bound for the slaughterhouse before we got them. My parents had moved out of the city in 1966 and bought a farm that ultimately became 130 acres. It had cattle, corn fields, and soybean fields. There was a back entrance and a country gravel road that led to a riding stable a mile away.

I had no desire to ride at first. My brother and sister would go riding, and I'd be out by the barn, playing in the dirt with my wagon. When I got bored of all that, I tagged along to the barn and started riding. The people across the road from us had horses. That's how it all began.

When we went to our first horse show, I didn't have any riding clothes. I had white jeans and cowboy boots. Compared to everyone else, we didn't have a lot. But I'm sure we were still better off than most. Anyway, in that first show, I won a class. People laughed at me for not having riding clothes, but the Brooks attitude is just to keep going.

From there, I kept riding. I remember I wanted a puppy that cost ten dollars, but I didn't have ten dollars. So, I went to the barn and said I wanted a job. I only had the white jeans and they got more and more dirty by the day. A few days in, the guy gave me my ten bucks and told me to get on out of there. I showed up the next day to finish the job.

"I thought that you'd leave when you had your money," he said to me. But I stayed until I finished the work he gave me. After that, he couldn't get rid of me. My family couldn't afford to buy horses, but the local trainer, Joe Racine, had a buddy, Bob Egan, with two horses he was going to send away. They talked, and the next day after school, our trainer came in with these two horses, and my dad wrote him a check for $55. My horse was smaller than my brother's, so we decided that mine cost $25 and his cost $30.

We had no bridles, nothing at all. The horses had those ski rope halters where you tie them into a knot.

We, of course, jumped onto those horses bareback and rode through all the fields that we farmed. A couple of days later, my mother took us to the North Manchester Tack Shop, and we bought our equipment. I remember my saddle cost almost $200. We had to purchase everything, even water buckets. We had been using the mop bucket from the kitchen to water our horses. One bucket. We didn't know any different.

We had two bales of hay or whatever Dad got from the neighbors. We would ride our horses—we weren't taking any lessons at this point—and every eight weeks, we would call the blacksmith, who would show up three weeks or more after that to shoe the horses. It was a big deal when he showed up. We were so upset if he came and shod the horses and we weren't there to watch. Heartbroken.

There was a new vet in town who had just graduated vet school, and he had a backyard horse who cost $250. My dad made a deal to lease the horse for $100 a year with an option to buy. As a kid, whenever I'd ask my mom questions, or bug her for something, she'd say "I'll think about it." So that's what I named the horse—I'll Think About It.

By then we were building jumps in our yard. We had eight acres of front yard. We didn't know what we were doing, and my horse hung his legs. Then I started hanging out with another friend and he began taking me to horse shows. It was a big deal. We slept in the truck and we were friends because of the horses. I was twelve or thirteen and he was five years older than me. Sleeping in the truck didn't bother me—I just wanted to go to the shows.

We had built stalls in our barn by this point, and the horses mostly lived out in the paddock behind the barn. I got a jumper next, named Dark Shadow like the TV show. My parents noticed that I took care of the horses, which was probably the turning point. My brother and I wanted to ride with these big-time trainers. My brother went off and rode with Sue Ashe and Otis Brown in Tennessee, and I rode with Russ Walther. And at sixteen, I was driving the horse van down the road. That's how it started, and next, I got a junior hunter loaned to me.

As a teenager, it was all about the gypsy life for me. Never living at home, always driving the truck, training horses. I thought it was glamorous—I didn't have a clue then. But I had my junior hunter, and by then I had my new pick-up truck. I also had rebuilt a two-horse trailer. I stripped it down to bare metal, sanded it, put a new floor in it, did the wiring myself. Paid a guy thirty bucks to paint it. Then, the day after high school graduation, my brother and I drove to California with my horse. Ever since then, I've preferred driving my own rig to horse shows. Even cross-country.

TRACI: I went to a day camp outside Cleveland in Ohio when I was about five years old and I learned how to ride. My mom tells a story about the parents' day at the end of the camp where parents could see what the kids had learned. They thought I'd be riding a little pony, but here I was, at five years old, on this giant horse, Alaska, having the best time. That's where it started.

My parents got me riding lessons and then a family at the stable offered to give me a pony because they were moving away.

"It's a free pony, we need to take it!" I told my mom.

"It's not free," my mom said. "It's not about the price of the horse, it's the monthly upkeep."

Lucky for me, my parents did agree to take that pony. His name was General Sherman. He was 14.3 (not a pony!) and he didn't change leads. When I outgrew Sherman, we got another pony. The new pony was green and taught me a lot. My parents were supportive and they did the best they could for not being horse people. They let horses be my thing and they dropped me off at the barn when I was old enough, and I'd stay all day on weekends. I couldn't get enough. I still have many of the friends made during that time.

I'd go to all the horse shows, even when I wasn't showing, just to be there all day and help. I did whatever was needed, whether it was holding a horse, wrapping legs, cleaning stalls, tacking or untacking. In those days, we didn't have grooms, so I learned a lot doing it all myself. I braided for a while, too (because my parents told me I was capable, and they didn't want to pay for it!).

I never had my own horse as a junior, but I catch-rode. I have a December birthday so I started school early, too. When I graduated, I still had one more year to show as a junior. I took a gap year before I went to college and got to ride that last junior year and show horses for other people. Mostly hunters, a little equitation, and even some jumpers. At all the local shows, I'd beg to "fill the medals" and people kindly found me horses to ride to do so.

Lucky for me, Cleveland—and the Chagrin Valley, specifically—was somewhat of a horse mecca. I was so fortunate to be surrounded by many amazing and well-respected horsemen.

From the start, I wasn't interested in doing anything else for a career. Even when I was in college, it felt a little bit like a waste of time—I could be riding! I knew that's what I was going to do. I wanted to be at the barn.

After school, I started working for a local trainer in Ohio. I was basically her rider. I got some really nice experience as a young professional, getting to show all the horses and helping to run the barn. Because the trainer had a young family, she had to stay home a lot. I ended up going to the shows by myself with five or six horses. I was the groom, the braider, the show rider, the training rider, and the trainer. I got paid forty dollars a day, plus my hotels. Forty dollars a day, and I thought it was the greatest thing ever! I would've paid her. And there I was cleaning stalls, braiding the horses, putting my riding clothes on, showing, coming back, putting them away, unbraiding the horses, wrapping legs.

Nowadays, I can be in our office and if a horse has a cut, I run out there and jump right into, "grab me this, grab me that …" I can see that sometimes our staff is thinking, "We didn't know she knew how to do that." But all those years of doing everything myself taught me so much. That's the real stuff. It's how you really learn to feel and understand the horses.

People started making comments: "If you can go to the horse show and do everything yourself, why not have your own business?" So, I ultimately took on a few of my own clients in Ohio. And then it grew from there. I did that until I moved to California. In Ohio, throughout my mid- to late-twenties, all my friends were getting married and having kids, and there I was, hanging out with my parents and their friends. I just thought: There is more than this. Plus, I was freezing during those Ohio winters!

My boyfriend at the time and his family were well-known Saddlebred trainers. They taught me a lot about long-lining, driving, and shoeing. The methods all crossed over because they're based on good horsemanship. We even put some of our hunters and jumpers in the jog cart! He ended up moving to Malibu and I went and visited a few times. I was hooked. I placed all my customers with appropriate trainers in the area and decided I'd move out to Malibu for six months, just to see how it would go. That's when I decided to take a break from horses.

I got a job in public relations and discovered what the rest of the world does on the weekends! I actually had the time to sleep in, to go out and do things, to live a whole other part of life. It only took about a month before I got bored. One day, I stopped by a local barn in Malibu and I met a trainer there. And I got sucked right back in. She started calling me, saying, "Hey, I'm going to be out of town, can you come teach my lessons?" We became good friends and she offered me the empty office at the barn, so I moved my PR office there. I'd do some PR, go ride a few horses, teach some lessons.

Pretty soon it started being more horses than PR. And then the trainer had a major family emergency. She asked me to take her customers to Indio (now Thermal). I went, and I brought a young investment horse I had as well. John French was there at Indio and he said to me, "Oh, you should show this horse to Carleton, he'll probably like it." That's how Carleton and I first met. I vaguely knew who he was because he used to come and show in Detroit and the Midwest when I also showed there.

Carleton was based in Atherton, California, at that time, and early in our relationship, I moved up there for about a year and a half. It was a bit of a rocky transition for us at first. I remember thinking: All this guy does is work! I later moved back to Malibu, where I began to work with Leslie Steele. It ended up being a great, important part of my career. I learned so much from her and we went on to work together for eight years and still do some today.

   Leslie is a true animal lover. She has many different kinds of animals, and she has great compassion for all of them. She understands animals, and I think that's part of why we get along—she puts herself in the animal's position and has a lot of intuition there. Her belief system is that everything starts with the comfort and health of the horse and treating each horse like an individual.

   While working with Leslie, via John French, I got the opportunity to manage a family's horses at their home in West Los Angeles. They wanted to share this amazing space they had created in their neighborhood with others. So I continued working with Leslie while also growing the West LA barn. Meanwhile, Carleton had closed his business in Northern California and was judging more. We spent more time working together on the business in West LA, which we still have today. We got married, and the rest is history!

   And as for the name Balmoral, people often ask about where we got it. Balmoral is the name of the street where I grew up, and where my parents still live.

CHAPTER 20
Through Each Other's Eyes

Traci on Carleton

I'VE NEVER MET someone more consumed with horses and with our sport than Carleton. He's obsessed, in the truest sense of the word. He'll be stumbling and bumbling down the hall, muttering to himself. I'll ask him, "Are you talking to yourself again?" He's always going over something in his mind or writing it down. It's his passion. And that's what makes him so good at it. He's always working to improve. His saying is that when you're figuring something out, you're going to fail nine times before you get it right by the tenth try. He'll say, "I screwed this up four times, so we're getting closer!" He just keeps coming back to it.

I always joke about his midwestern work ethic, too. He doesn't know how to be idle. The only way he knows how to relax is when he's driving the horse van across the country. Because he's sitting still. But he's still working, and so he doesn't feel any guilt about it. I wonder, "Why does he like driving across the country? He doesn't want to drive closer to home with the horses. But he'll drive on the open road." I think that it's relaxing for him. As much as he's able to relax, anyway! In the beginning it was hard to get him away. He's gotten better over the years about going on vacation and not getting antsy. It's still not easy, but I know it's good for him to recharge so, while it's rare, we do our best to get away on occasion. When we plan our time away together, it can be for a week or even just a few hours. Working together and being married is a balance and we're careful to schedule enough time together.

I think one thing that people don't know about Carleton is that he is so compassionate and a big softie. He's the opposite of what people might assume about him. He's the most sensitive person, which I think makes him good at what he does. He really reads into the horses and just feels it. Sometimes he might even have a harder time with people because he's so in tune with the horses—just super compassionate, in touch, and sensitive, so it can be a bit harder for him to interact sometimes.

When it comes to our business together, we have a division of duties. We listen to each other and trust each other completely. Every day is different, and every hour is different, and there are so many decisions that need to be made; if we didn't trust each other, we wouldn't be able to do it. When there are big decisions, we discuss them. But we both make a hundred little decisions a day on the fly, and because of our mutual trust and respect, it works.

We pick our battles. We have a lot of discussion-type meetings. We try to put our phones down at some point. I think that when two horse people are married and run a business together, it's similar to actors. When an actor is married to another actor, they understand the lifestyle. I think that's super helpful. Things are also moving so quickly in our lives that we almost don't have time to let emotion come into it, which is good! We don't take things personally. We keep it positive and we keep moving forward.

As for buying horses, we don't question each other. We trust each other 100 percent. I might call Carleton and say, "I bought a horse off a video today." And he's like, "Okay." Of course, there are times when we're tested, and times that we want to challenge each other. I think we both have good intuition—which you need to have if you work with animals.

I also think we complement each other well because I'm a very glass-half-full, optimistic type, and Carleton is very detail-oriented and pragmatic. I'm more of a big picture person—I say yes and figure it out later. He's more of a devil's advocate. (I tease him about that!) He's thinking about the worst- to the best-case scenarios, and I'm always thinking of the best-case scenario, and somehow we end up weighing all the options and meeting in the middle, so it works for us!

Carleton on Traci

I can't say enough good things about Traci. I can hardly express how fortunate I am. When we show in the desert each winter, there are 3,000-plus horses on the grounds, and Traci and I are in different areas of the showgrounds for most of the day: Divide and conquer. But whenever we're in the same general area and I finally get to see her, I have the biggest smile on my face. I'm so fortunate.

When I decided to dive deeply into this business again, I didn't want to do it by myself, and I think I found the perfect partner.

What Traci brings to the table balances me out so much. With her input, things become so much clearer and our students get the maximum benefit. I find it amazing.

I worked at this for twenty years as an individual and wished I could fill in all the voids; it's such a feeling of completeness now because of her. We approach things from different viewpoints or different sides, sometimes, and I think that benefits our horses and riders.

It's a very unique situation, and we are able to build stronger, from the base up, working together.

We have an understanding with one another about trusting the other person's decisions. Little, split-second decisions happen all day long, and sometimes they end up making a big impact. So, it makes the most sense for us to just trust one another at every turn. We back each other on the small decisions, and also on the big ones, like buying horses.

People also may not realize that Traci is riding every single step with our riders. She's exhausted at the end of the day, because she "rode" as many horses as she had lessons.

Traci has compassion and empathy for everyone. And she wants them to realize that what we teach is a process. To trust the process. And Traci knows the process.

CHAPTER 21
Working in the Hunter Jumper World

WE ARE INCREDIBLY lucky to get to do what we love for a living. It always starts with the horse and our love for horses—building a life around them is truly rewarding. However, to be successful in this business, you have to realize that the horses are a small piece of the puzzle. They are much simpler to manage than humans! It's the people, the administration, and the organization that are the hard parts. Absolutely key to a well-run business is finding people who are good at more than just the horses and the riding. Surround yourself with a great staff, pay them well, appreciate them, and listen. Good people are hard to find. When you're fortunate enough to find one, hire and create a position for them. You won't regret it.

Working students and young professionals have to be willing to pay their dues. It's not all about the riding—riding is just one small part of working in

> "The horse business is hard. Life is hard. When difficult situations arise, I like to ask myself: Will this matter in a week? A month? A year? A lot of people have asked me how I stay so positive. The truth is, I didn't actually realize that I was! But I do live and work by these tenets: Keep a good attitude, keep moving forward, keep showing up." —TB

170   WITH PURPOSE: THE BALMORAL STANDARD

> "I was at one of the jumper rings in Thermal, heading back toward the hunter rings. An older gentleman was slowly walking by and I asked if he'd like a ride somewhere. He thanked me kindly for it and got in the golf cart. 'No one else would have done that, so, thank you,' he said. I think the horse show culture needs to realize that we have to be there for each other. A lot of people have been raised to believe 'to each his own.' But I don't think that works. The only way we've become successful is because other people have reached out to us. Now we need to give it back. Tenfold. Whether you think you do or not, you always have time to be nice." —CB

this industry. You have to be willing to get up early, stay up late, freeze, sweat, not have days off, be wrong, ask questions, and be wrong again. These jobs are not for the timid!

Because working in the world of horse shows is such an all-encompassing endeavor, the burnout rate is also very high. People often ask us the secret to not burning out in this industry, and the truth is ... we don't know! Maybe it's going out to dinner. Seriously, though, getting away from this insular world, just for a bit here and there, restores the balance. We schedule time away and time together.

Not placing all the emphasis on results, but enjoying the process to the results, is also key to making this work. We can't help but be results-driven, but we're also production-driven. It's about having realistic

LEFT: Balmoral's David Vega (center, pictured at Devon) won the WCHR David Peterson Trophy, awarded to a person who exemplifies dedication and commitment to the care and well-being of horses, in 2020.

> "On a Sunday during the Desert Circuit, at the end of the day, this older couple walked up to me and asked where to go to watch. I pointed them toward the Grand Prix ring, but as they walked away and I hurried off to another show ring, I thought, 'That didn't feel good.' This couple must have read about the Grand Prix in the newspaper or something. I whipped around in my golf cart, found them, and said, 'I'm going to take you. Get in.' I took them in the VIP, sat them at our table, and organized lunch for them. Carleton and I talk a lot about how that's the stuff that's really important." —TB

expectations, managing those expectations, and realizing everyone's definition of success is different. Each person's journey and experience is unique.

Working in this industry is about the whole journey. It's the relationship with the horses, the relationships with the people, it's watching the horse come along from where it starts to where it ends up. And these kids who have their version of success. That doesn't necessarily mean winning. We have one young rider for whom just cantering around a course is a great accomplishment. For one of our older adult riders, winning is cantering bravely to the single oxer. No matter how you define a win, they are all measures of success. And one isn't better than another. Celebrate your victories, however small you think they are. Because you're brave for getting out there!

While we're on the subject, to us, teaching that older adult rider is no less gratifying than teaching the rider who is going to show at Indoors. It's always about the individual. The walk-trot kid, the junior showing at Thermal, and the adult who's afraid but keeps showing up. We're teaching them all, and no one is more important than anyone else. When they have a good day, it's a good day for us. That helps keep everything in perspective.

CHAPTER 22

On Judging

HERE'S OUR UNDERSTANDING of how horse shows got started. Each family on a farm or an estate had horses. They bred more horses, and then they started to make challenges.

"I have the prettiest horse."

"No, I have the prettiest horse."

"Well, let's get together and have a party. We'll get so-and-so, who's supposed to be an expert, and they can decide whose horse is prettier."

Class after class got added and horse shows took shape. You would go from estate to estate with your horses and these parties, and that's how it all began.

HORSE SHOWS TODAY

People love to ask what a judge is looking for. Most judges' first impression of a horse and rider is dependent upon cleanliness and presentation. And a good presentation comes from well-fitting, traditional items.

Here's how we see it: Every judge is different. Every class is different. Generally speaking, depending on the quality, conformation, and suitability to the job, each horse picks up the canter in the ring with its own base score. Some start with a 9, some start with an 8. The very best, or the ideal, start from a 10.

> "I remember one year at Indoors, a friend and well-known hunter judge stopped me on the ramp and she said, 'You should clearly be winning these classes, but you're second or third. What are you going to do?' I told her, 'I'm going to keep my chin up and I'm going to keep going.'" —CB

The horse's pace and track weigh heavily on a judge's score, as well as the horse's movement and its jumping style. Don't forget how little time you actually spend jumping. An over fences class is also judged on what the judge sees between the jumps. After all, that's what produces brilliant jumps in the first place. But it is a jumping contest!

Horse showing is like anything else. The more you do it, the more comfortable you will get, and the more you will ride at ease in the show ring. Your performance will show grace and beauty more than tension. If you only drive your car once in a while, you won't be as comfortable as you'd be if you drove often. There's a comfort level that you express to the judge that only comes with time and repetition.

You can never forget that this is a subjective sport (jumpers notwithstanding). The judges are doing the best job they can to be fair and place the horses in the correct order. What the judge sees is a matter of perspective, literally, because they are in a fixed position outside the ring. Your perspective, on your horse, is much different from the judge's. Therefore, you may feel like you don't agree with the placings at times, and you may

> "I ride every single horse I judge. The whole trip. I'm exhausted at the end of the day. It's 170 trips, sitting there. People may not realize it, but I'm riding that horse right along with you." —CB

feel like you got a gift at other times. We like to think it comes out even in the end.

As an example, we recently had one of our amateurs come out of the corner and her horse took maybe half a trot step on the way to the single oxer. This particular judge didn't see it, or perhaps they didn't count it as a trot step. And our rider caught a gift, as reflected in her score. But that will balance out some other time when she'll feel she got shortchanged on her score or her placing. The more you show, the more these things average out, and you'll feel that you're being fairly judged as a whole. It's all going to come out in the wash over time. The more you compete, the more you tend to feel that you're being judged well. It's a numbers game.

In classes where the round gets a numerical score, there tends to be a curve with judging. On one day, there might be a lot of scores in the 90s, which certainly makes a class fun to watch. The judge still puts the class in the right order, it was just on a higher curve.

Numerical scoring can be hard for people to grasp sometimes, but we think that focusing on the curve more so than the number can be helpful.

> "When a rider gets a 76 but they think it should have been an 84, I always say, 'Did we accomplish our three things we set out to do in this round? Yes? Then it's a good day.' The judge didn't know what three things we were working on. If you did what you set out to do in that particular round and you got a 76, you passed. And you've got something to build on for the next time you walk in the ring. It's all building blocks. It's the process." —TB

Sometimes you win with a 90, sometimes you win with a 76. It's about the order, not the number.

Even when there are numbers involved, it's still subjective. Think about a rider who gets an 84 one week, and a 76 the next week. It's the same horses in the class both weeks, and the rider comes in third both times. In that case, it doesn't really matter what the number is, right? That horse and rider were the third best of the pack each week. Whether the score is 84 or 76 is inconsequential. Just because there are numbers involved doesn't change the fact that we don't have standard deductions in the hunters. Flow, smoothness, and the overall feeling of a round all come into play in scoring, as does the judge's personal preferences for the way each horse goes. Numbers or not, judging hunters is always subjective.

The judge doesn't expect to see you ride perfectly, but they do expect to see

> "I've always looked at it like this: If we can consistently be in the top end of the results, we're solid. If we're champion or reserve or knocking on the door week after week, that is achieving the high end of success. We don't try to win all the classes. Someone told me recently, 'We were champion, but we never won a class this week.' That's the ultimate. They were that consistent. I'd rather be solid round after round than win one out of ten." —CB

how you handle the little things that come up on course. The judge expects you to make adjustments—just not abrupt, rough adjustments. Everybody tries to be flawless going into the ring. But that's actually when you're supposed to make adjustments. It's like a dance. It's about when you choose to make those adjustments and how that will make a difference in the overall picture.

That beautiful, smooth round never quite feels that way when you're riding it. You're feeling every step, every little nuance. As you're going around, you're going through your checklist and making little adjustments as needed and then it ends up looking great. If you make a lot of minor adjustments, you shouldn't have to make a major one.

We tell our riders, especially with our adults, 'You can't be attached to the outcome. It's not within your control.' And then we go back to the three things the rider is setting out to do on any given course. Whatever that person is working on, if they accomplish those things in a round, that's a win for them. It makes it quantifiable, too, when a rider can check those boxes. Building on that, the wins will come.

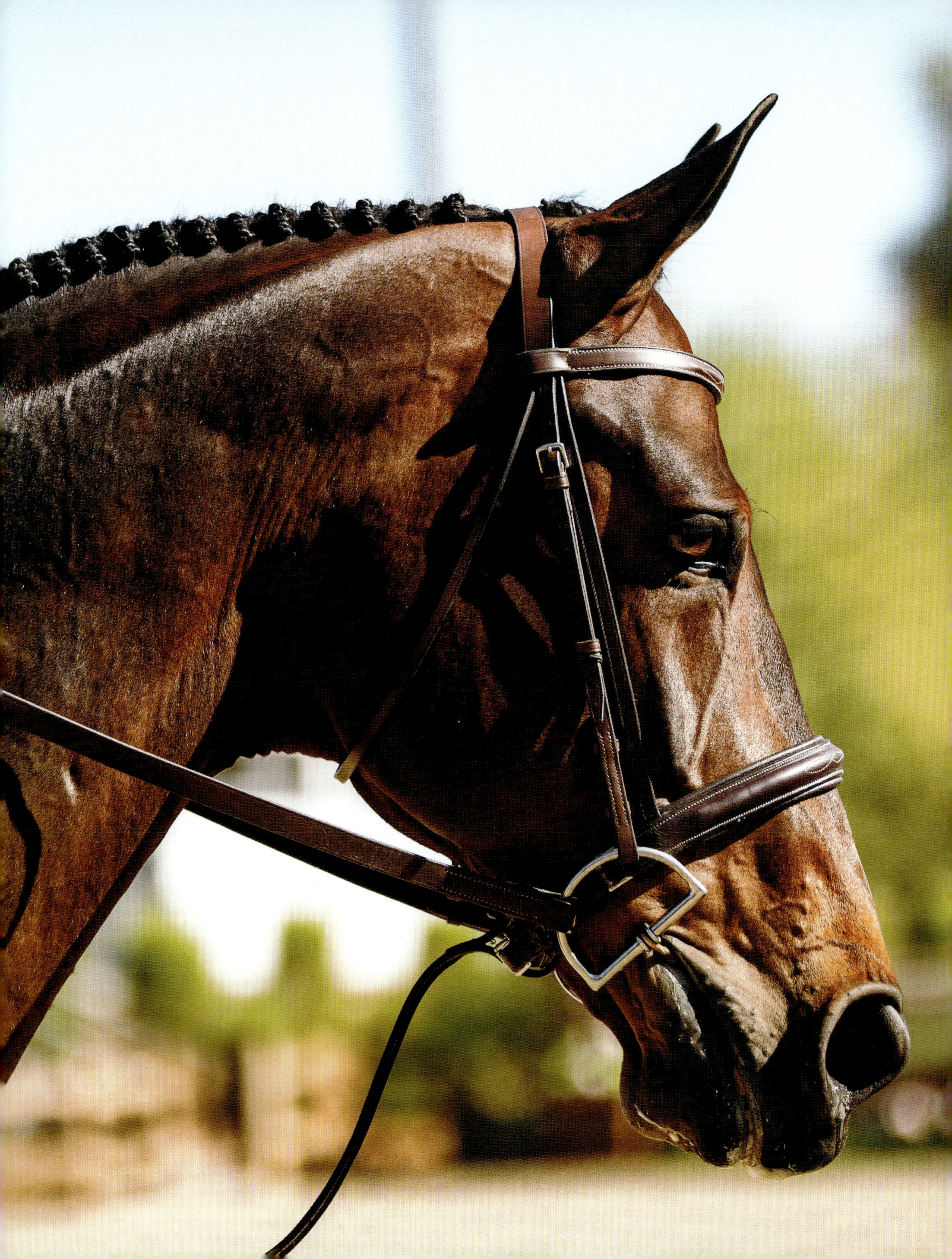

CHAPTER 23
Horse Insurance

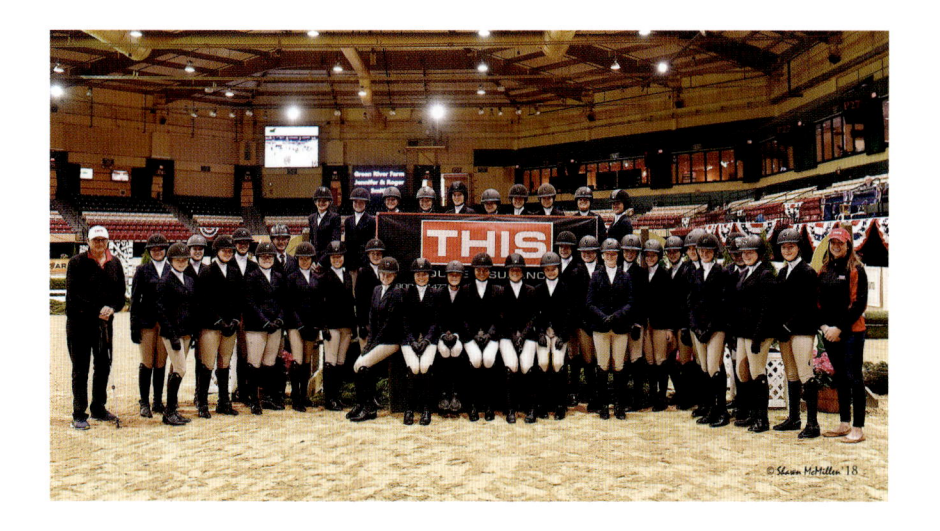

IF YOU'RE NEW to horse ownership or leasing, it can be overwhelming to learn all of the costs involved. After the purchase or lease price, there's board and training. Then you've got basic farrier and vet charges, showing expenses, plus any maintenance work necessary for your particular animal—like vet maintenance and possibly acupuncture, massage, and chiropractic work—and then you've got insurance. For many who are newer to the sport, this can be initially viewed as just another expense on a long list of expenses. But it's a necessary one that, in some cases, will end up saving you a lot of money. More importantly, buying insurance for your animal is a way to purchase peace of mind. Unfortunately, sometimes horses get sick or they get injured, and those vet bills on top of the usual expenses can really add up.

We asked our good friend Michael Taylor, of Taylor Harris Insurance Services to write this chapter for us. We believe it's important that everyone who owns or leases a horse or pony understand the basics of insurance. We love and respect Michael, his company, and his support of the industry.

Insuring Your Horse or Pony
By Michael Taylor, President of Taylor Harris Insurance Services

When you consider what people understand about horse insurance, it varies from zero to a whole lot. We've got the entire spectrum out there. My goal in this chapter is to provide a simple education in insurance for people who buy or lease a horse or pony.

Horse insurance is an intangible. And when you are buying horse insurance, you're really buying a promise to provide another intangible—peace of mind. An insurance agent's job is to explain to a horse owner or lessee exactly what they're buying, how much it costs, and give that person many options as to what might suit their program the best.

There are a lot of new people getting into this sport, and it can be difficult at first to truly grasp the cost of participating. No matter what your level, horse ownership is expensive. And horse insurance is a cost that needs to be added

> "I'm an insurance agent for Taylor Harris Insurance Services myself. Carleton and I looked at it as an opportunity to be closer to the source and to be able to provide an added service to our clients. In addition to trusting us with everything about their horse or pony's care, a client can go through me directly to insure their animal and be privy to how this sometimes-confusing piece of horse ownership works." —TB

into the equation. It's not a substantial cost compared to what you pay the trainer or the vet, but it's a crucial element to consider. At the end of the day, insurance will, at the very least, protect your investment. At the most, it could save you great sums of money.

When people call us and say, "I have so much to learn about insurance," they've come to the right place. My agents will start from the beginning and the client will end up truly understanding what they're getting. It's a relationship, and our agents get to know both the clients and their animals. One of the advantages of being a specialized, niche business, is that you can actually talk to people. In the old days, when you went to the bank, you spoke to someone in the bank. Nowadays, you're much more likely to speak with a computer. With horse insurance, you'll actually speak with someone who can talk to you about your horse. I believe that is one of the most important things we do.

We're in the horse business too, and we're always cheering on our clients. It's personal. And if your horse gets hurt, that's personal to us, too.

YOUR HORSE'S VALUE

So, let's begin with the basics. When you insure a horse, you are protecting the investment you've made on the animal's life—we call this mortality. It's not uncommon to have new clients say that they want to purchase major medical coverage (to avoid paying unexpected vet bills out of pocket), but not mortality. However, mortality is the one non-negotiable when it comes to horse insurance. One way to think about it is that you need to insure the whole before you can insure the parts. The whole is the living, breathing animal. Once its mortality is insured, then you can move on to the parts, like major medical, or other à la carte coverages.

The first determination we make when securing mortality is the horse's value, which is based on the purchase price. Say you purchased your horse for $50,000. We can insure the animal for $50,000, but you can also insure the animal for less than the purchase price. That's a personal decision, and everyone is different. Only you know what will provide you with peace of mind at the end of the day, and your insurance agent will help guide you through that process.

Here's where it gets interesting. Over time, if the animal does grow in value—say you light the world on fire and end up champion at every horse show—you can call your insurance agent and discuss increasing its value. A value increase above the purchase price is primarily based on the show record. So, unfortunately, you can't call up and say, "Well, I believe my horse to be worth $200,000, so that's what I'm going to insure it for." Your insurance agent is there to help you protect the sum of money that you invested into your animal. And adjustments can be made from there if applicable.

MEDICAL AND OTHER COVERAGES

After we establish the mortality value, then we can add separate coverages, like major medical coverage or surgical. We can talk about territorial limits, so if the horse is in Europe, we can cover it for the time abroad for an additional premium. Or if you buy a horse in Europe, we can cover it for the plane ride back to the US. There are a lot of different supplemental coverages on top of that mortality.

For example, let's say someone calls and tells me, "I have this new horse, and I'm going to be financially devastated if it has to have colic surgery." If colic coverage is important to you—and it's one of the most common things that happens to horses, even if we do everything correctly—then we can add on major medical coverage. A major medical plan is not going to cover routine things like joint injections or vaccinations, but if something significant happens, that's when major medical will help you out.

The specific amount of medical coverage varies between underwriters. The term for horse owners and lessees to be familiar with is "limit of liability." That is the maximum amount your insurance is willing to pay regarding medical bills. Anything over the limit of liability would be your responsibility. At Taylor Harris, our underwriters offer three tiers of coverage on medical limits: $7,500 limit of liability, $10,000 limit of liability, and $15,000 limit of liability.

The value of the horse will determine the amount of medical coverage available to you (remember: we insure the whole first, and from there, determine how to insure the parts). If you have a $40,000 horse, all of those three options would be available to you. If you have a $12,000 horse, you could purchase the $7,500 or the $10,000 limit of liability. Like any other area of horse insurance, when you have a gray area or a question like this one, that's when you have a conversation with your agent. They are in the business of helping you understand your options and choosing what's right for you.

As far as paying the premium on your policy, all of our policies are issued on an annual basis. Monthly or quarterly payments are also an option if a customer prefers not to pay the entire year's premium up front. And as long as there are no claims, the policy can be cancelled at any time pro rata (meaning you only pay for the days you use).

EXCLUSIONS

Sometimes, there are conditions in the horse that are pre-existing to the policy which would not be covered. If a horse has had a previous surgery, for example, that would be excluded on the policy. If the horse has had an episode of colic without surgery and your insurance paid a claim on that, you'd also have an exclusion. However, if the horse doesn't have a re-occurrence, we can always go to the underwriters and ask for the exclusion to be reviewed. Outside of major surgery, there can be a fluidity to exclusions.

This is where we circle back to horse insurance being such a personal business. Exclusions are examined on a case-by-case basis, and there is always time to have a conversation with your agent. (If only things like health or car insurance were so personal!)

LEASING VS OWNING

If you're leasing, you're essentially taking on somebody else's big investment, so insuring that horse or pony is crucial to protecting yourself financially. Major medical insurance on a lease horse protects the lessee from being stuck with big medical bills, and the mortality coverage protects the owner in the event of a total loss.

For someone new to having their own horse, leasing can be this wonderful adventure, except for that scary realization of, "If the horse seriously hurts itself, do I have to pay an exorbitant amount of money?" That's where major medical kicks in. And if the horse were to pass away while out on lease, the owner is the beneficiary of the mortality value.

Insurance can work both ways on a lease. If someone wants to lease me his horse, that owner may add me to his own insurance policy, and ask me to pay the insurance premium. Or, the owner might ask me to take out the policy as the lessee, and include his name on the policy as the beneficiary as well. Those details are typically discussed while drawing up the lease agreement. In every scenario—from the first-time horse owner, to the more seasoned horseman who wants to learn the best ways to insure their investment—we are a personal business first. Each horse is different, each owner or lessee is different, and we're here to accommodate and provide you with peace of mind about your animal.

And that peace of mind, we believe, is priceless.

*For further details, please visit THIShorseinsurance.com.

CHAPTER 24
Team Balmoral on Carleton and Traci

DAVID VEGA, ROAD MANAGER AND HEAD SHOW GROOM:

CB and Traci are great human beings with big hearts. They love horses and all animals—it just runs in their blood! They are very dedicated to what they do, all day, every day of the week. For Traci and CB, today starts yesterday or a day before. Like CB says all the time, "think ahead."

I've worked with CB for twenty-five years. He is an amazing rider, trainer, and most important, he is a real horseman who cares about horses and ponies all the way around. CB is one of a kind. He's the full package, so good with the horses on the ground in addition to the riding. He likes a challenge, he doesn't like easy things. He likes to work for them. I think that'd be his middle name—Challenge.

MIGUEL ESCALANTE, BARN MANAGER, HEAD GROOM:

Traci is always ready to give her all in training, working harder than anyone. She is truly a multitasker—there's no job she can't do. It's incredible how she handles everything with a smile, always making sure the horses are good and ready to show.

It's amazing how Carleton always walks into the barn with a smile, trying to make everyone happy. He looks at each horse to make sure they're good in

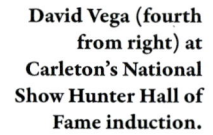

David Vega (fourth from right) at Carleton's National Show Hunter Hall of Fame induction.

every way. He is not just a boss, he is a friend, always trying to lend a hand for whatever anyone needs. And he's always willing to teach anyone who's willing to learn about horses.

R SCOT EVANS, R JUDGE, CLINICIAN, BALMORAL TRAINER-AT-LARGE:

Carleton and I have known each other since we were teenagers, so I've witnessed his development over the years into the horseman that he is today. Here is what I know for sure: While being competitive and always striving for the best performance in the show ring, most of all, Carleton is coming from a place of what works best for the horse at any particular moment. I believe that the horses—and his dogs—pick up on a heightened level of compassion and empathy from him. There are many times when he will be in deep thought and it's always about how to make the horse comfortable and happy in their job.

Traci and I immediately connected with our teaching techniques in simplifying things through small steps with the riders. I often find her connecting with the junior and amateur riders in a way that makes them feel confident in themselves simply by being around her. Traci's passion stems from her love of horses and the joy that the sport brings to the riders.

JEAN WINGIS, ASSISTANT TRAINER:

Traci and CB have been at the top of their game for as long as I've known them, and they show no signs of slowing down. Their combined knowledge and experience, balanced with love and humor, create the perfect environment for developing great horses and successful riders.

As someone who teaches for them while they are on the road, I rarely see the dream team in person, but I do see their imprint on every aspect of the program. The horses are wonderful. They shine with good health and are happy to do their jobs, thanks to the dedication of the talented riders and grooming staff. They arrive at the ring early and immaculately turned out. No detail is overlooked.

The students arrive prepared to work hard and to learn. They are kind to their horses and supportive of one other. They are serious and curious and a pleasure to work with. I'm often stunned by the improvement in their skills and confidence when I haven't seen them for just a week or two. The Balmoral culture of giving 100 percent every day comes from the example set by Traci and CB, who never give anything less.

HOLLY HIGGINS, FORMER ASSISTANT TRAINER:

CB is one of the few people I've worked with who watches the horses in the stalls as well as in the ring. He watches how they move, which legs they're favoring, how balanced they are, how they're eating, whether they're tight in their gut. He'll look a horse up and down and say something like, "That horse's heel is too low." He's looking at the whole conformation, while most people focus on the riding. You can learn so much just looking at a horse.

There's a horse whisperer element to Carleton. He's the last one standing, I'd say. Most people now want to focus on the riding, and any kind of shortcut. He is one of the last real horsemen in the hunter jumper world. So many people just get lost in the showing.

The real proof comes in that every horse he walks up to is happy to see him. They love him. You'll see it with the dogs, too. Animals really like him. And it's hard to maintain that connection to the horse. It's the industry part of it. If this is your job, people get jaded. But he manages to come in every day with fresh eyes. He's obsessed. He'll stay up all night thinking about one thing with the horses. All night. And then in the morning, he'll say, "So, now I think we should try this." It's great to see someone at the top of this sport bring that level of enthusiasm and energy to it, day after day, year after year.

Traci's compassion is one of her best qualities when it comes to training horses. She really loves the horses and helps them to be at their soundest, fittest, and happiest. One of her best qualities for training riders is her ability to break a concept down and simplify it. She has a great way of teaching riding that allows people to understand what they need to do to get the desired reaction from the horse.

Traci comes to work with a fresh perspective every day. Her enthusiasm for teaching and helping horses and riders is truly refreshing. She particularly loves teaching children and matching them with ponies and horses that instill confidence and love for the sport.

DINO FRETTERD, CHIROPRACTOR:

I've been in the horse world for twenty-six years and I worked for a lot of people. Passion is the very first word that comes to mind when it comes to CB. Holistic. Horseman. But more than anything, Carleton has the passion. He's got common sense, he wants to do right by the horse, and he wants to teach and to educate.

If you're not passionate about something, then you're mediocre at it. It's not his decision to do anything mediocre. Anybody who knows CB is going to tell you that mediocre is not in the equation for him. It's not a variable. It doesn't exist. It's not in the vocabulary. He doesn't settle for anything less than what he feels should be the best. For his horses, and for the people that work for him. A great example is David Vega, who's been with him for almost three decades.

CB is all about paying attention to details. He's being a good horseman. He is one of a kind. And with his passion comes skill, knowledge, horsemanship, patience. And a willingness to share all of those things. Teaching you to learn patience with the horse. That's a quality that most people don't have.

The horses love him because he loves them. Horses are more telepathic than we are. Much more attuned to their environment. They have to be, it's just instinct. Horses just know. And they know how much CB loves them.

Copyright © 2022 The Plaid Horse

Library of Congress Control Number: 2022918340
With Purpose: The Balmoral Standard/Carleton Brooks and Traci Brooks

ISBN: 978-1-7329632-8-3

WARNING

Horseback riding is an inherently dangerous activity that could result in possible serious injury. This book contains general techniques and information that may not be suitable for all readers. Employing a qualified professional instructor is recommended for all who wish to participate in equestrian sports.

Cover photos by Kind Media LLC
Book Design by Caitlin Choi

Photo Credits

Lindsey Long Photography (p. 2, 3, 4, 8, 11, 15, 18, 22, 27, 28, 29, 30, 39, 43, 44, 49, 54, 58, 66-67, 70, 71, 72, 73, 77, 78, 99, 112, 117, 118, 120, 122, 128, 143, 146, 149, 156, 162, 165, 177, 178). Sara Shier Photography (p. 6, 12, 25, 334, 36, 51, 52, 53, 54, 55, 64, 71, 74, 75, 76, 85, 88, 89, 91, 94, 112, 122, 124, 126, 133, 164). Adam Hill, Ph.D. (p. 12, 19, 21, 34, 50, 65, 79, 92, 95, 96, 97, 113, 115, 116, 123, 143, 176, 182, 186, 187). Irene Elise Powlick (p. 16, 98, 150-151, 189). Piper Klemm, Ph.D. (p. 22, 104, 169). Shawn McMillen Photography (p. 32, 35, 46-47, 127, 179). Traci Brooks (p. 42, 170). Kind Media (p. 78, 87, 90, 124, 143, 149, 166). The Book LLC (p. 103, 155). Andrew Ryback Photography (p. 53, 60, 83, 135). Brooke Marie Photography (p. 56, 62, 68, 71, 74, 75, 141, 174, 177). Jennifer Taylor (p. 151, 152). Photos courtesy of Traci & Carleton Brooks (p. 59, 84, 88, 100, 101, 104, 105, 106, 107, 108, 109, 110,111, 121, 123, 128, 129, 130, 131, 134, 137, 139, 140, 144, 152, 153, 154, 157, 158, 159, 160, 161, 171, 172, 177, 188). Cathrin Cammett (p. 95, 100, 107, 120, 125, 144, 177). Forever Photo Company (p. 41, 102). Joseph Norick (p. 168).

Printed in China